BUILDING AN OUTREACH SUNDAY SCHOOL
A Lessons for Life Manual

BUILDING AN OUTREACH SUNDAY SCHOOL

A Lessons for Life Manual

JILL MASTERS

Child Protection Policy Appendices
CHRIS COOPER

THE WAKEMAN TRUST, LONDON

BUILDING AN OUTREACH SUNDAY SCHOOL

© Jill Masters 2005

THE WAKEMAN TRUST
(UK Registered Charity)

Website: www.wakemantrust.org

UK Registered Office
38 Walcot Square
London SE11 4TZ

US Office
300 Artino Drive
Oberlin, OH 44074-1263

ISBN 1 870855 44 2

Cover design by Andrew Owen

Printed by Stephens & George, Merthyr Tydfil, UK

Enlarge, inflame and fill my heart
With boundless charity divine:
So shall I all my strength exert,
And love them with a zeal like Thine;
And lead them to Thy open side,
The sheep for whom their Shepherd died.

Charles Wesley, 1707-88

BUILDING AN OUTREACH SUNDAY SCHOOL

Contents

CAN SUNDAY SCHOOLS SUCCEED TODAY?
A Personal Note

SUNDAY SCHOOLS for children, where they still exist, tend only to cater for the children of believers. Even in American all-age Sunday Schools the children's classes are usually drawn from churchgoing families. The old concept of a local church taking spiritual responsibility for *all* the children and young people living in its neighbourhood has almost disappeared. The devastating results of this policy are now to be seen all around us.

Many Christians maintain that even if an evangelistic Sunday School were to be held, today's children would not be interested or persuaded to attend. Yet I have gained the impression over the years that there are thousands, even millions, of children who would attend Sunday School, if only churches were to seriously operate evangelistic Sunday Schools, obeying the command of the Saviour to suffer little children to come to Him! I hope readers will forgive a little personal reminiscence to show how I came by this impression.

As a child of parents who had given up church attendance I myself was collected every Sunday afternoon by teachers from a local evangelical church in suburban London. My parents were glad to have a few quiet hours on Sunday and had us ready for the collector's welcome knock soon after lunch. In early days I heard about the

Saviour and was drawn by the cords of His love to follow Him. This Sunday School later opened a branch in the community centre of a large nearby London housing estate where I was privileged to serve as a young teenage teacher. Hundreds of children flocked along over many years. Even the local ice-cream van man saw his opportunity and greeted the children as they left at 4 o'clock. At times the hall, which held over 200, was too small and the problem was how to avoid sending children away. The great majority of these children came from families living in the surrounding flats, whose parents never attended church. What a tragedy it would have been if this opportunity had been missed!

My next positive experience came in my early twenties as a pastor's wife in a church being pioneered in a new town north of London. Secondary school premises were hired for use as a Sunday School venue. Letters were distributed in the neighbourhood announcing the start of a Sunday School, followed by a personal visit to most homes. On the first Sunday, 73 children turned up and soon a thriving work was under way. Within no time the attendance passed the 100 mark. Not one of these children was from a Christian home, yet they attended regularly on Sundays and at the weeknight meeting which was later started for them. Two coaches had to be hired to take them on the first Sunday School outing. The numbers of children attending helped persuade the local authority to lease the fledgling church a site for a building. In the course of time, parents and even grandparents, contacted through means of the Sunday School, attended the adult services regularly and an evangelical church flourished in that town.

This second experience confirmed my view that many children were ready and waiting to come and consider the Gospel if only Christians made this possible for them.

From a smart new town where our church building was surrounded by bushes and bluebells, my path led to the huge church building of the Metropolitan Tabernacle in central London, an area known at the time for its violent youth gangs. Would a serious, traditional Sunday School cut any ice here? Would children growing up on crowded estates be allowed to come and learn the Ten Commandments and the way back to God? They certainly would not have come had we only sent an invitation and waited for them to appear, but instead a 'retired' Devon country-bus was purchased by the fellowship to ferry children to and from their homes.

Children like to be with a crowd, so in order to rapidly increase the numbers an 'Easter Mission' was held for a week in the school holidays. Our green bus was driven through the estate where invitations had been distributed to parents, and over 100 children gathered that week, leading to a large jump in the regular Sunday attendance.

Here in central London (and the same would probably apply to other cities) this provision of transport has proved to be, under the Lord's hand, the great key to success. Those who continued to organise the different bus runs (17-seat minibuses are now favoured) have commented that if Christians are willing to go and knock on doors and provide transport, then 'the sky's the limit' to Sunday School attendance. How sad that such opportunities are missed.

The other vital component of the work was the substance of the Sunday School hour, necessary for maintaining the children's interest and attendance. At that time almost all the materials available in the UK were unsuitable for us, being aimed at children from Christian homes who were assumed to be 'little Christians' already. To meet the need for lesson notes that would be chiefly evangelistic (but also teaching doctrines), I began to refine and extend notes I had prepared for our new-town Sunday School, and 'Lessons for Life' gradually came into shape. Teachers also took care to provide suitable, challenging visual aids.

With the prayers and labours of the church membership we had the joy of seeing hundreds of children attending Sunday School each week in the years ahead.

Over the years we have also revived two branch Sunday Schools in this part of south London. One branch often exceeds 100 children in attendance, and the other exceeds 50. Recently another church in a nearby area moved its Sunday School to the afternoon and soon reported an increase of over 100 children in a very short period of time.

Articles in Christian journals have often written off Sunday Schools as failures, but we can testify to the fact that we now have many members, including many young people, who have come up through the School. At the time of writing over thirty of the present Sunday School teachers are former scholars, and others of their compatriots are serving in Sunday Schools around the country. We now have Sunday School 'grandchildren' attending. An increasing number of former scholars (of all ages) are returning to worship and seek the Lord after having seen through this present world.

Our highest concern is the Lord's glory. It is His wish that 'every creature' should hear the Gospel, so that He will rightly ask on the great day of judgement, 'What could have been done more . . . that I have not done?' *(Isaiah 5.4.)* While such a door of opportunity stands open, should we not take it? There are doubtless places where for some reason the children simply cannot be drawn to Sunday School, but my personal experience seems to suggest that there are still large areas of Britain today which would yield great fruit if only labourers would move into the harvest field.

A TOUCH OF HISTORY
When Did Sunday Schools Begin?

Since the Reformation, child evangelism and instruction have been a priority for Christian people. Luther and Calvin wrote key catechisms and instructionals for children, and their high degree of concern was taken up by succeeding Protestant churches. We know that many of the English Puritans gave much time and attention to specific instruction of the young, all this taking place in times when the entire population, with children, attended the house of God. But as compulsory churchgoing declined, and cities began to grow, a huge non-churchgoing underclass emerged. Happily, however, with the Great Awakening of the 18th century, God's people, moved with compassion, thought of the children, and ragged schools and Sabbath Schools sprang into existence. Some of the great names among Sunday School founders are Hannah Ball (who started hers in 1769), John Newton (1770 – actually a Thursday School), Robert Raikes (1780), Rowland Hill (1784), Thomas Charles of Bala (1789), and John Rippon (c. 1801). In 1784 John Wesley reported that he found Sunday Schools springing up wherever he went – stirred into being by the heartbeat of revival. Amazingly, by 1831, Lord Shaftesbury was able to say that one-and-a-quarter million children attended Sunday Schools in Britain.

What Sunday Schools Used to Look Like

An insight into the past may be gained from the work of teachers at the Metropolitan Tabernacle years ago. In 1875 (during the ministry of C. H. Spurgeon) the Sunday School had more than 1,000 children in regular attendance (not counting those at branch sites), of which 150 were in senior classes. In addition to this, there was the famous girls and young women's Bible Class led by Mrs Bartlett, attended by between 500 and 700 every Sunday.

Furthermore, branch Sunday Schools at the Tabernacle's mission halls added another thousand children – Richmond Street Mission having 650, Green Walk Mission, Bermondsey 350, with other branch schools attracting hundreds more. The records of the Tabernacle prove that very large numbers of members (over many generations) were brought to the Lord through the ministry of its

Sunday Schools. The great majority of these converts were gathered from godless homes in their early years, and would never (humanly speaking) have been likely attenders of a church or chapel but for the outreach of the Sunday School.

Remarkably high numbers continued until just before the Second World War when the main Tabernacle Sunday School roll reached 1,500 children and the seven branch missions added over a thousand more. And these were not the only evangelical Sunday Schools in inner-Southwark. Until the outbreak of war, Sunday School attendance throughout Britain followed a similar pattern, that generation of scholars providing the backbone of churches for decades to come.

How different it is today! Sunday Schools have been disparaged by a new generation of ministers since the 1950s. Comparatively few children now experience the loving concern of the Lord's people. Few learn the principles of the Gospel – or even basic moral values – from Bible-believing churches. Many children in central London today have never opened a Bible. The vision to reach entire communities has died in the hearts of present-day Bible Christians.

Section 1
WHY START A SUNDAY SCHOOL?

1. What is the Purpose of a Sunday School?
2. The Benefits of an Evangelistic Sunday School
3. Why Evangelise Children? – A summary
4. Are We Guilty of Child Neglect?

1. What is the Purpose of a Sunday School?

A Sunday School is a place . . .

- where as many children and teenagers as possible are gathered from the district to win them to the Lord, not merely to instruct children of church members;

- where children receive weekly evangelistic Bible lessons in which they are shown their sinfulness in God's eyes and His wonderful provision of a Saviour;

- where children are taught to worship, pray and listen to God's Word;

- where a serious, structured course of Bible learning from Old and New Testaments is presented in a captivating manner by a team of committed teachers, supervised overall by the church leaders;

- where an annual programme of events, some related to the 'church year', provides teachers and children with opportunities to relate together in the context of Christian example;

- where a Christian atmosphere is available to children living in a godless age, including a weeknight gathering (to encourage those who attend on Sundays) with recreational activities and devotions;

- where the heart and witness of the church fellowship is invested in the preparing of a living church for decades to come.

2. The Benefits of an Evangelistic Sunday School

- Sunday School enables a church to fulfil the great commission as found in *Mark 16.15*. How else can we reach and challenge modern youth?
- Sunday School plants the Gospel seed over time in a large number of hearts, ready for the Spirit to germinate, some sooner, some later.
- Sunday School provides us with an opportunity to deliver children from the future pain and shipwreck so often inflicted by the permissive society, shielding them from the worst excesses of sin, and imparting standards to consciences.
- Sunday School provides friendly contact with homes to which we would never otherwise gain access (including homes where there are drug and alcohol problems, criminality, and other church-alienating factors).
- Sunday School gives fulfilment to the members of the church, providing avenues of important service for many.
- Sunday School contributes much to the development of a happy, spiritually healthy fellowship with few assurance problems, and little strife, because many members share a vital Christian service commitment. (The wonder of the Gospel is best appreciated by those who teach it.)
- Sunday School leads to a band of saved young people who can 'fish' for others.
- Sunday School attracts to the church Christian families who are keen for their children to have its instruction.
- Sunday School identifies and inspires future pastors.

3. Why Evangelise Children? – A summary

- The Lord Jesus Christ commanded this *(Mark 16.15)*.
- Children are often more open than adults to the Gospel message and are the most fruitful field for evangelism *(Mark 10.15)*.

- Scripture and church history demonstrate that the Lord has often called His choicest servants in childhood years.
- Children have their whole lives before them, either to be lost in sin or to be lived to the glory of God *(2 Timothy 3.15)*.
- The future of the church and its witness is in the saving of the children *(Psalm 78.6)*.
- The Saviour has said He particularly wants children to come to Him *(Matthew 19.13-15; Isaiah 40.11)*.
- Through children we can reach into homes – to their parents and other family members *(2 Kings 5.2-3)*.
- God has promised to bless those who evangelise children *(Isaiah 44.3-4; Matthew 18.5; Mark 9.36-37; Luke 9.48)*.
- Children can die while young, and need to be prepared for eternity *(Revelation 20.12)*.

4. Are We Guilty of Child Neglect?
by C. H. Spurgeon

'Many professing Christians ignore the multitudes of children around them, and act as if there were no such living beings. They may go to Sunday School or not; they do not know, and do not care. At any rate, these good people cannot trouble themselves with teaching children. I would earnestly say, "Do not sin against the child by such neglect." "No," says Reuben *[of Joseph in the pit]*, "we will look after him when he is a man. He is in the pit now, but we are in hopes of getting him out afterwards." That is the common notion – that the children are to grow up unconverted, and that they are to be saved in later life. They are to be left in the pit now and to be drawn out by and by. No word of Holy Scripture gives countenance to such a policy of delay and neglect.'

In the next section this book changes gear to deal in a very practical way with the details of Sunday School work and organisation. The advice and tips offered embrace the needs of very large Schools, but those 'starting small' should not be put off. We must begin as we can, and the Lord will bless.

Section 2
PREPARING TO START

1. The Stance of the Church

Prayer and dependence on God are vital *(Psalm 127.1)*. Building a Sunday School is a long-term commitment by the church which can only be sustained by the help and empowering of the Lord. Special prayer meetings for the inauguration of a Sunday School are vital.

Materials, music, venue and staff must be considered carefully. The pastor and officers of the church should be closely engaged in the decisions leading up to the launch of the work and its subsequent development.

The teaching syllabus must be based on the Word, carefully planned and structured in order to ensure purpose, unity and soundness. The pastor and other elders who have ultimate responsibility for the quality of teaching in the church should propose or scrutinise materials to ensure that these are sound and suitable. Sadly, many good churches are using unsatisfactory materials which often contradict their own doctrinal beliefs. New evangelicalism has made great headway into children's literature. Others are using lessons which are boring and predictable and not likely to win the interest of the children. Some have scant Gospel content and treat lightly the all-important subjects of sin and the need of a Saviour. Trivial, entertainment-style materials may keep children amused for an hour, but will not earn their respect or teach them the way to Heaven. There is a great danger that far from leading them to God, these materials will bring them to scorn Christianity.

A whole-church project. The entire membership should ideally have their heart in this work. The Sunday School will provide opportunities for Christian service in many ways, not just in teaching (see section on staffing on p 23).

A coordinator will be required (more often called the superintendent) the selection of whom needs much prayer and guidance. We prefer the 'coordinator' term as the 'superintendent' should strictly be the pastor, or other appointed elder. The Sunday School, after all, is not, and should never become, an independent department.

2. Government Legislation for a Child Protection Policy

Some churches known to us have felt intimidated by government legislation about the care of children, and have recoiled from re-opening or enlarging their Sunday Schools. They have apparently been told by well-meaning but mistaken advisors that they would have to implement impossible precautions and rules to satisfy the law. The law does not bind churches to unreasonable 'standards' as some think, but requires churches to have a stated policy for children's work, which includes certain provisions. These sensible, safe and workable details are set out in Appendices 1-3 entitled 'Discipline and Child Protection Policies'. Nothing in this policy should inhibit the building of a large Sunday School.

3. The Best Time for Sunday School

We recommend that serious consideration be given to an afternoon School as the preferred time, although we recognise that occasionally 'local wisdom' may point to another time. Non-Christian families in many areas are more likely to be ready to come out in the afternoon. Larger numbers of believers are free in the afternoon to staff the Sunday School adequately and to collect and return children from the neighbourhood safely to their homes, a great incentive for non-churchgoing parents to send their children. When the School is placed immediately before a morning service, or alongside it, staff are not usually available on the scale required.

There are more likely to be opportunities in the afternoons for those who return children to their homes to speak to their parents.

Some churches hold 'Sunday School' on a weekday evening or on Saturday, but this has the drawback that the children are not helped to see the special nature of the Lord's Day.

4. The Building

Parents need to feel safe in sending their children to Sunday School. In the case of a pioneer School, *a prominent, well-known building* will help to assure parents. A church hall or a school or community hall is ideal.

A clear and attractive sign on the door or close to the entrance is authenticating and welcoming, giving parents the confidence that this is a properly organised and safe place to send their children.

Aim to develop a large crowd. Movable screens are useful for adjusting the room to suit the numbers present and can be moved outwards as the numbers grow. Fill seats from the front, leaving no empty seats. Have extra available in case they are needed.

The *welcoming registration desk* needs to be clearly marked and adequately staffed to cope with the arrival of the children a few minutes before the start time. It needs to have a supply of cards to list new children's names, ages, addresses and telephone numbers and, if applicable, the name of the person who collected them for Sunday School.

Make certain the necessary arrangements are in hand to ensure that the hall and classrooms reach the *correct temperature* when children arrive, especially in winter. Young children from poorer families often come quite scantily clad.

5. Equipment Needed

A supply of Bibles – children could be awarded a Bible after several weeks' attendance (six weeks seems about right).

Musical instrument – ideally a piano or a keyboard, but avoid instruments associated with latest worldly trends. Automatic 'midi' players for electronic keyboards are now available at modest cost, with a full range of hymns and choruses, so the lack of a proficient pianist is not an insurmountable problem.

Hymn board, sheets, or overhead projector – books can be expensive and easily damaged. Words on coloured card add a bright dimension. Sheets and lists of hymns are available from the Tabernacle Bookshop. These can be laminated and used for many years.

Chairs – stacking or folding for easy removal. Small chairs for the youngest children are easier to handle and save space.

Boards – white or black, for displays, visual aids, etc. The old-fashioned easel can be moved about and stored with ease. Liquid chalk sticks add quality and remove the dust problem.

Items for reward schemes – star charts and text tokens leading to small, novel prizes are beloved of children and inexpensive.

Screens (as used in offices) can be used to provide 'classrooms' in a single hall. Those with castors are recommended so that they can be wheeled into place at lesson time and removed when a whole department is together.

Registers – a 'new children's register' to record full details of a child on his or her first attendance. Also department registers so that the performance of the whole group can be seen at a glance. Also class registers so that teachers can use these to:

- check the children's attendance and visit when absent;
- pray regularly for each child;
- remember their birthdays;
- keep an accurate record of attendance so that prizes and rewards can be awarded fairly.

A *supply of folders or pouches* – not essential, but these will encourage children to take their *Bible Learning Course* leaflets seriously (see p 39).

A *bell* – the old-fashioned brass school bell brings a group to order in a friendly way.

A *coat-rack* where children can safely leave outdoor clothing.

A *photocopier,* or PC with a fast printer, is most useful for the work of a Sunday School, enabling the School to coordinate and improve communications, and, of course, to copy take-home leaflets for children and advice notes for teachers.

First aid – first-aid facilities in a place known to all the staff should be regularly restocked.

6. Staffing – the Many Posts to be Filled

If the School grows in size, the following workers will be needed, but do not be put off. Many churches, especially new causes, will start small, and may only have two or three workers. Here is the ideal:

Teachers – soul-winners willing to be evangelist and pastor to the young, with a heart and an ability for communication.

Collectors – ready to go out weekly in all weathers to knock on doors and bring in the children, some by foot, others in vehicles. (This is an unmatched missionary opportunity, providing a friendly acceptance with many homes.)

Drivers – to drive church minibuses. These must possess a clean driving licence and a good reputation for responsible driving (fuller information is shown on page 75). A church officer should be appointed to verify that they are safe drivers. A transport coordinator will also be needed when a number of people are actively engaged in bringing children in, to organise routes and personnel, maximise the efficient planning of routes, and to ensure that church vehicles are kept in good running order. (See Section 7.)

Visitors – Teachers themselves are the best people to visit their children, including absentees, but a team of recruiting visitors to build up the numbers constantly is a vital asset. The size of a Sunday School depends greatly on the amount of visitation carried out.

Registrars – (one for each department) are needed to keep clear, accurate records of all new children (their name, address, date of birth) and of the weekly attendance. (See p 79.)

Helpers/Stewards/'Policemen' – Many discipline problems can be avoided if people are available to spot problems before they occur, and to recognise and befriend potential troublemakers.

Pianists – In days when hymn-singing is often a new experience for children, the pianist will play an important part in the children's worship (see 'musical instrument' under Equipment Needed, on p 22). Timing is very important. Hymns may be sung a little faster than for the adult congregation so as not to be dreary, but they should always maintain reverence and give children time to think about and mean the words.

Artists – The happy, yet God-honouring atmosphere of the Sunday School will be raised by graphics and illustrations of a high standard. PCs provide smart lettering wherever needed.

Cooks – will be needed on several occasions to provide meals and 'treats' for special events such as the Sunday School party.

'Bookkeeper' – To save the church treasurer time, a reliable person can be appointed to hold a 'float' and reimburse the comparatively small expenditures incurred by Sunday School staff. He or she can then present the account when needed. Larger outlays will need to be referred to the treasurer.

Medic – a person who has first-aid training or a doctor or nurse who will themselves be available at the children's gatherings or outings.

Motor mechanics – Precious funds can be saved by those who are willing to do basic maintenance on Sunday School vehicles. If vehicles are kept smart, bearing the Sunday School 'logo' in a window they will earn the confidence of parents (and are less likely to be broken into).

Shoppers – A scheme for giving small rewards (see 'text tokens' on p 28) to children makes a helpful difference. Those good at spotting a bargain and prepared to keep the stock of sweets and novelties will do a service to children and teachers alike.

Furniture movers – In order for a Sunday School to operate smoothly, all items of furniture and equipment need to be in place well before the children arrive. Often the School shares the use of its hall with other church activities and a team of volunteers who can move chairs, screens, etc into place makes a vital contribution to the work.

7. Sunday School Classes and Departments

Allocation of children to classes will vary greatly depending upon the number and ages of children and the availability of teachers and classrooms. While the Sunday School is small or constrained by space it will probably be wise for the whole School to meet together for the first half of the proceedings (not using departments), and then separate into classes for lessons. As soon as it grows, departments can be established.

In general it has been found best to follow the pattern of day schools for division into beginners (pre-school), infants, juniors and seniors and, as the School grows, year groups. These boundaries are respected by parents and children. In Sunday School boys and girls often prefer to be taught separately from junior age upward and this enables moral teaching to be more personal.

Most volunteer teachers will do best with the age group for which they have a preference. More experienced teachers would normally be expected to handle older classes, but don't underestimate the skill needed for the youngest.

A visual aid pinboard with a colourful wallpaper frieze will provide an attractive focal point in hallway areas pressed into service as classrooms.

8. The Opening Day

- Consider a good time to begin, perhaps in early October when holidays are over and most children are settled in day school. Churches have found it helpful to hold a weekday Bible club during the school holidays to gather a crowd of children just before or after opening a Sunday School. But care must be taken not to allow the club to drain enthusiasm and effort from the Sunday School project which is more important and longer lasting.

- Make every effort to start with as large a number of children as you can manage. A crowd draws a crowd.

- Enthuse church members to bring their own families, neighbours' children and school friends.

- Visit the neighbourhood with well-presented invitation cards or letters a week or two beforehand.

- Make personal visits to the homes during the previous week to answer queries and encourage the children to come, taking details of those who wish their children to be collected.

- Provide a team of adults who will call for children on the day and bring them to Sunday School, either walking with them or using Sunday School transport (see Section 7). All should carry a means of identification.

9. Sunday School Invitation Literature

Give the name of the church, its address and telephone number with a picture of the Sunday School building if possible. Include the name of the pastor or Sunday School coordinator.

Sample points to make –

- Sunday School is held (for example) every Sunday from 3-4pm.
- Newcomers are always welcome to join the many other boys and girls who attend. No charge is made.
- It may be possible for children to be collected – ask our visitor.
- All children join a class which is specially designed for their age group with its own regular teacher.
- All teachers are members of the church and have received Sunday School training.
- Each week the children receive a lesson from the Bible. The Sunday School follows the *Lessons for Life* four-year, structured course of lessons.
- Children will receive a weekly Bible Learning Course leaflet which will indicate what they are being taught.
- Children who attend regularly are invited to the weeknight meetings (give day and times) during school term time, when children enjoy a time of recreation with an epilogue on a moral and spiritual theme.
- The church operates a Child Protection Policy in accordance with Government guidelines.

Note: An additional card carrying Sunday School information is extremely useful, and is described on p 79.

10. Incentives to Sunday Attendance

The following incentives have proved to be a great help in encouraging children to attend Sunday School regularly. They are not bribes, but legitimate ways of rewarding attendance and good behaviour with items which children appreciate, and which are of modest cost.

Sunday School Bible. When children first come to Sunday School, they can be given a small card on which a star is placed each week. After six attendances, they are given a Bible, treasured by most children. Once they possess their own Bible they can be encouraged to bring it weekly, and also to follow the daily readings given on the Bible Learning Course leaflets available with *Lessons for Life* (see Appendix 4).

Text tokens. This is a simple reward system which has been successfully used by Sunday Schools for generations. Small cards printed with the church name and a Bible text are awarded by the teachers. Children may, for example, receive one text token for attending, one for bringing their Bible, and one for completing and returning a Bible Learning Course leaflet. They may also be given for successful answers in quizzes. A text token stand is operated at the close of the Sunday School hour, where the tokens may be exchanged for simple stationery items, small books, toys or sweets. Children love to collect text tokens (almost as if they were banknotes) before exchanging them for prizes. Teachers will need to agree on a policy for awarding the tokens so that the system is fair throughout the School.

Weeknight meetings (see also p 93). In the past, many churches operated a weeknight meeting for the young. These meetings might consist of an hour of games, cooking or other young people's activities, followed by a half-hour of devotions including a serious evangelistic or spiritual-interest talk lasting around 20 minutes, which strongly supports the Sunday work. (Weeknight meeting notes are available from Tabernacle Bookshop.) At the Sunday School of the Metropolitan Tabernacle, children are expected to attend Sunday School on a regular basis in order to be admitted to the weeknight meeting for their age group. These are not used as a bait or springboard to Sunday School, rather the other way round. They are very popular.

Prizegiving. Prizes for attendance through the year and for Scripture memory work should be given at an annual prizegiving meeting. The prizes will usually be Christian books. The special meeting is a real incentive to the young and provides an opportunity to invite parents who love to see their children receiving prizes. (See p 84.)

Annual events. Certain annual events such as the winter party and the Sunday School outing are of immense importance to the children and are often spoken of months in advance, and for years after! They can be a great help in maintaining regular attendance, especially at times of the year when numbers flag, and add colour to the Sunday School calendar as well as providing teachers with an opportunity to get to know the children better. (See Section 8.)

Section 3
ORGANISATION

1. The Sunday School Coordinator

(Until the Sunday School grows, the work of coordinator and department leaders may be carried out by the same person, or the pastor or an elder may act as coordinator with a team of leaders.)

Qualities, Gifts and Circumstances Needed

A strong sense of mission in seeing the need for and the possibilities of child evangelism. A love for children and particularly their souls.

A sincere regard for the teaching team, and an ability to organise the assignment of teachers to classes in a spirit of happy agreement, and also to advise and inspire teachers.

An informed understanding and affirmation of the faith as held by the church so that wrong teaching and methods will not creep in through the Sunday School, making its work counterproductive.

A willingness to consult closely with, and observe the direction of, the pastor and officers as the entire ministry of the church is ultimately their responsibility. It is essential that the coordinator appreciates that while his/her suggestions and experience will be vital, yet final decisions must be in the domain of the pastor and elders in the choice of lesson materials, and in the appointment of staff and speakers.

A clear gift in organising a growing, many-faceted organisation. At the start a Sunday School coordinator may have to wear many hats and single-handedly take on the work of recruiter, collector, organiser, teacher, registrar and home visitor. In time and with the Lord's blessing, the role may include the management of a large staff and a complex programme of events.

The Chief Responsibilities of a Coordinator

He or she will need to:–

- inspire a team of workers for the great work, set the standard of commitment and spot the potential of church members for the varied tasks needing to be done;
- propose leaders and teachers for each department, for the approval of the pastor or elders;
- provide a structured outline for the Sunday School hour (see p 66 for a suggested order of service), gently making suggestions for improvements as the work develops;
- train new teachers by holding classes at a convenient time, and allocating trainees to learn and work alongside experienced teachers until they are ready to take their own classes;
- be closely involved in the running of all departments so as to notice potential problems before they develop, and take steps to solve any which arise without causing rifts;
- maintain standards throughout the School, helping in the provision of materials, artwork, and literature and making useful comments on any proposals by department leaders;
- keep in constant view the main School registers, checking the attendance figures to ensure that visitation is maintained, and action taken (such as a recruitment drive) as soon as any decline is noticed.

2. Organising the Sunday School Year

The Annual Plan of Lessons

Where a Sunday School is using *Lessons for Life*, the coordinator can plan the year's lessons in advance and provide teachers with the year's calendar. The *Lessons for Life* system is tailored to fit around the Sunday School year. Most Sunday Schools, like day schools, will divide their programme into three terms a year. Most will want to break from regular lessons and substitute special topics at Christmas, New Year, Easter and perhaps other holidays and special occasions. Speakers usually choose and prepare their own subjects on these Sundays, and it is therefore assumed that a maximum of 46 lessons are required each year. The lessons are grouped into series, and individual Sunday Schools may use these in any order to suit their Sunday School year. However, the Old Testament series should be kept in chronological order, whereas New Testament series may be fitted into the year according to choice.

The Annual Timetable of Sunday School Events

Beside the lesson plan, the coordinator will organise the year's events. The concept of a Sunday School year helps give coordination and security. Sunday Schools may wish to follow the day-school year, which in the UK begins in September. On special Sundays class teaching is set aside and each department remains together in class time to be addressed by a special speaker (this is called 'open school' – see p 86 for suggestions). This could be one of the most experienced and capable regular teachers or a 'visitor' from within the fellowship (eg: an officer) or an outside guest speaker.

A Sample Calendar — allocation of lessons using *Lessons for Life* Book 1:

5 Jan	New year text[1]		30 Mar	EASTER DAY, Open School	
12 Jan	Lesson 1	SERIES 1: MARK'S GOSPEL I (Miracles)	6 Apr	Lesson 12	SERIES 3: MARK'S GOSPEL II (Opposition to Jesus)
19 Jan	Lesson 2		13 Apr	Lesson 13	
26 Jan	Lesson 3		20 Apr	Lesson 14	
2 Feb	Lesson 4		27 Apr	Lesson 15	
9 Feb	Lesson 5		4 May	Lesson 16	
16 Feb	Lesson 6	SERIES 2: GENESIS I (In the Beginning)	11 May	Lesson 17	
23 Feb	Lesson 7		18 May	ANNIVERSARY, Open School	
2 Mar	Lesson 8		25 May	Lesson 18	SERIES 4: ACTS I (Journeys of Paul)
9 Mar	Lesson 9		1 Jun	Lesson 19	
16 Mar	Lesson 10		8 Jun	Lesson 20	
23 Mar	Lesson 11		15 Jun	Lesson 21	

22 Jun	Lesson 22	SERIES 4:	
29 Jun	Lesson 23	continued	
6 Jul	Lesson 24		
13 Jul	Lesson 25		
20 Jul	Lesson 72 Rich Fool[2]		
27 Jul	Lesson 73 Lost Coin[2]		
3 Aug	Open School		
10 Aug	Open School		
17 Aug	Open School		
24 Aug	Open School		
31 Aug	Last lesson with classes[1]		
7 Sep	Promotion Sunday[1]		
14 Sep	Lesson 26		
21 Sep	Lesson 27	SERIES 5:	
28 Sep	Lesson 28	GENESIS II	
5 Oct	Lesson 29	(God's Great	
12 Oct	Lesson 30	Plans)	
19 Oct	Lesson 31		
26 Oct	Lesson 32		
2 Nov	PRIZEGIVING, Open School		
9 Nov	Lesson 33		
16 Nov	Lesson 34	SERIES 5:	
23 Nov	Lesson 35	continued	
30 Nov	Lesson 36		
7 Dec	Lesson 37		

14 Dec	Lesson 75 Lost Sheep[2]	
21 Dec	CHRISTMAS SERVICE,	
	Open School	
28 Dec	Open School	
4 Jan	New year text[1]	
11 Jan	SERIES 6: JOHN'S GOSPEL	
	('I am' Sayings)	

[1] Lessons to be devised by the teachers themselves.

[2] When a series of lessons ends only a week or two before the end of term, to fill the gap we suggest borrowing lessons from a series where each lesson is a separate entity (eg: the Parables, in Book 2). It is best to wait until the beginning of the next term before starting a new series (especially when this is an historical series). Remember to omit these individual lessons when the series is taken up in a future year.

A Sample Year – with items needing advanced planning in small type

The plan below includes two 'new years' – the calendar new year in January and the secular day-school new year.

January: NEW YEAR MOTTO TEXT – prizes are awarded to the children who hand in the best coloured-in text sheets. WINTER PARTY – an opportunity to have a happy time together on a winter Saturday.

Make arrangements for Easter and Anniversary speakers. Decide on destination for summer outing, book venue and transport.

Easter: REMEMBER THE LORD'S DEATH and resurrection; open school in departments.

Make detailed arrangements for anniversary and outing.

May: ANNIVERSARY – an annual special Sunday. Invite a speaker for each department, also children's parents and friends. Arrange a display of visual aids, children's work and photographs of Sunday School events to interest visitors and win support. A special opportunity to present the Gospel to all.

July: SUMMER OUTING – a day out together – never to be forgotten!

Collect information about teachers' holiday plans and prepare a roster for the August holiday period. Cover for pianists on holiday is important. Consult department leaders about staffing requirements and changes for the new Sunday School year in September.

August: OPEN SCHOOL (during school holidays) enabling teachers to take a holiday while their classes are in abeyance, and enabling children to take a holiday without missing curriculum lessons. All benefit from a change from the normal scheme, so that the new term in the autumn is eagerly anticipated.

Produce list of staffing arrangements for the new Sunday School year. Sunday School teachers are volunteers so care and personal consultation are needed. Prepare a list of books which can be recommended for the prizegiving.

September: AUTUMN RECRUITMENT – during the last week of school holidays and the first week of a new Sunday School year. Invitations to be distributed on a larger scale around the neighbourhood. Arrangements need to be made for collection of interested children, etc (see p 78). PROMOTION WEEK – new Sunday School year begins. Visiting of scholars to ensure that all are back for new term. New registers must be ready for new classes. Learning of annual memory work verses begins.

Registrars to provide a list of children who have won attendance prizes with the record of books given to each child in previous years, so that duplication does not occur. Organise a selection of prizes (usually chosen by class teachers), labels for books, and programme for the prizegiving afternoon.

November: PRIZEGIVING – annual event, rewards for attendance and for successful memory work. Another special Gospel presentation.

Make arrangements for special speakers for Christmas service, if held. Also the Sunday School may like to send a card inviting parents to adult services.

Select a New Year text and arrange for this to be printed and at hand for the first Sunday in January.

December: CHRISTMAS SERVICES – open school – remember the Incarnation. Present a card and small gift. Open school on the Sunday following Christmas – *remember* God's faithfulness through another year and consider the new year ahead – the opportunity to seek and find Him, to serve Him and to experience His blessing.

Section 4
TEACHING MATERIALS
The *Lessons for Life* Plan

1. The Aims of *Lessons for Life*

Lessons for Life lesson notes have a threefold aim:

First, they have an *evangelistic aim,* using selected Bible portions which are clearly intended for evangelistic application. Each lesson seeks to confront children with a true understanding of the truths and arguments which, under the Holy Spirit, lead to conversion. They avoid children being left with a mere familiarity with Bible 'stories', and aim instead to lead them to the path of salvation. Our first desire is to lead children and young people to a saving knowledge of the Lord Jesus Christ (see p 47).

Secondly, they are intended to give a *good outline knowledge of all the Scriptures.* The syllabus (see pp 41-42) seeks to deal with Bible events in an orderly manner, worthy of the Word of God. The Old Testament is mainly dealt with chronologically, so that the pattern of God's dealings with mankind before Christ is known and appreciated. In this lesson scheme, the Old Testament series are interleaved with the Gospels and *Acts.* Both children and teachers prefer this method of following a basic historical pattern, to those approaches which jump from one part of the Bible to another with such frequency that all perspective is lost. Each week this scheme provides another instalment in the great plan of God. Pastoral needs of young believers can be catered for, so that parents (unbelievers as well as believers) will appreciate that their children are receiving a structured biblical education.

The third aim of these notes is *to present challenging spiritual topics to the minds of the young.* The very plan of the Bible suggests themes which may be highlighted in our teaching. For example, the early chapters of *Genesis* offer an opportunity to present a serious challenge to the whole evolutionary/atheistic outlook; the book of *Exodus* presents the theme of life as a journey or pilgrimage; and the lessons from the latter kings of the Old Testament facilitate a number of apologetic arguments from archaeology, vindicating the Bible as the Word of God, proven and trustworthy. *Luke's Gospel* is divided into two series – the parables, and a catalogue of conversions entitled, 'People Who Followed Jesus'. *John's Gospel* lends itself to an easily remembered series on the great 'I am' sayings of the Lord. A stirring, historical account of Christ's life is followed from *Matthew's Gospel.*

By such lessons we aim to offer the children a varied Gospel challenge as they set out on life's journey. Prayerfully, our concern is that these will lead them to the Saviour in early years, but if not, that there will be in their minds and hearts a knowledge of the Lord which may be used by His Spirit in later years to prick their consciences and lead them to seek the Saviour.

Many published lesson schemes provide graded, separate notes and worksheets for each age group. *Lessons for Life* adopts a different policy. Experience has shown that teachers are the best people to adapt the lessons to each individual class. The notes therefore contain material which may easily be shaped to the needs of all age groups, from Beginners (pre-school age) to the teenage Bible Class. A range of suggested applications and guidelines is provided so that teachers may utilise the points most suited to their age group. Teachers of older classes often use the complete lesson outline, while those teaching younger classes select fewer points. In the many years this scheme has been in use in large numbers of Sunday Schools, feedback has shown that teachers are very happy to 'grade' the lessons for themselves. (See 'Hints for Teachers of Younger Classes' on p 51.)

2. *Lessons for Life* Bible Learning Course Leaflets

These take-home leaflets accompany each lesson. Printed on A4 sheets, they contain an outline picture for colouring by children, daily Bible readings based on the week's lesson, questions, a key text to colour, and a hymn verse which may be used as a prayer, inviting children to respond to what they have learned.

They are produced so as to be useful to a wide age group and very inexpensive. They may be freely photocopied from provided masters for local use. Parents (including those who do not attend church themselves) have told how they follow the Bible readings daily with their children. The fact that they follow the portion of Scripture covered in the previous Sunday's lesson means that the children will understand the words and fully appreciate that their teacher's message came from God's Word. Children can be encouraged to follow and complete the four-year course by being issued with a suitable folder or case in which to collect the sheets. Marks and prizes may be awarded as they complete each section.

3. The Purpose of *Lessons for Life* Visual Aids

In addition to the visual aid suggestions in each book, a series of full-colour visual aids have been published to accompany *Lessons for Life* books. These are designed to:
- endear the great Bible events and characters to the young with bright, friendly illustrations for every lesson;
- promote respect for the Lord and His Word (avoiding trite, amateurish illustrations);
- help avoid dull, predictable presentation and application;

- capture and sustain children's interest and curiosity through the lesson with 'hidden' words and surprises;
- present important information (maps, genealogies, etc) in a clear, attractive, easy-to-remember style (freeing teachers to concentrate on vital, spiritual issues);
- link lessons in a series with a theme visual aid (often larger than the regular aids) to form coherent, memorable clusters of lessons (eg: the Lord's 'I am' sayings from *John's Gospel*, Mediterranean ports in Paul's journeys);
- save teachers time by providing ready-made visual aids and freeing them to visit the class, prepare lessons, etc.

Each lesson has two or three A3 (42cm x 30cm) gloss card sheets of pictures, cut-out words, and in some cases clip-together displays, to captivate the curiosity and interest of children. Packs contain over 90 sheets (with easy-assembly instructions). Top-quality professional artwork serves to make these aids compelling to a generation of children accustomed to sophisticated graphics. (None of the visual aids contain pictures of the Lord.)

They are printed on robust 200 and 250gm gloss card and should stand up to use over repeated four-year syllabus cycles. The cost of a year's visuals is below the cost of most other Sunday School systems, yet they are of exceptionally high quality.

Art folders with clear plastic A3 wallets, available now at a reasonable price in stationers, can be used to store most of the cut-out visual aids so that a year's supply can be stored in a quickly recognisable order.

4. The *Lessons for Life* Four-Year Syllabus

Lessons for Life 1 (lessons 1-46)

Miracles Demonstrating Jesus' Power (Mark's Gospel – Part I)
The Lord's saving power seen in His power over nature, death, the devil, human need and illness (5 lessons)

In the Beginning (Genesis – Part I)
The truth about God, creation and the Fall, with the earliest salvation testimonies (6 lessons)

Opposition to Jesus (Mark's Gospel – Part II)
Examples of key sins – prejudice, pride, hardness, hate, etc – seen in the Lord's opponents, and to be repented of by all (6 lessons)

Highlights from the Conversion and Preaching Journeys of Paul
(Acts – Part I)
Evangelistic lessons from the life (and converts) of the apostle (8 lessons)

God's Great Plans (Genesis – Part II)
Character studies from Abraham to Joseph showing the power and goodness of God towards His people (12 lessons)

The 'I AM' Sayings of the Lord Jesus (John's Gospel)
Exalting the Saviour through His own great metaphors – the Living Water, the Bread of Life, etc (9 lessons)

Lessons for Life 2 (lessons 47-92)

The Christian Pilgrimage – Salvation from Sin's Slavery
(Exodus – Joshua – Part I)
The journey from Egypt to Sinai (8 lessons)

People Who Followed Jesus (Luke's Gospel – Part I)
Christian conversion and its chief characteristics (11 lessons)

The Christian Pilgrimage – Pictures of Salvation and Heaven
(Exodus – Joshua – Part II)
The journey continues from Sinai to Jordan (6 lessons)

Gospel Appeals in the Saviour's Parables (Luke's Gospel – Part II)
Teaching the consequences of sin and the only way of escape (11 lessons)

Judgement and Deliverance (Joshua – 1 Samuel)
Examples and warnings for all, from Rahab to Saul (10 lessons)

Lessons for Life 3 (lessons 93-138)

Gains and Losses in Following Jesus (Mark's Gospel – Part III)
Repentance, faith and conversion, and their alternatives (8 lessons)

Great Differences (1 Samuel – 2 Chronicles)

Contrasts drawn from the lives of David and Solomon to illustrate conversion and the believer's privileges (12 lessons)

Early Reactions to the Apostles' Message (Acts – Part II)
Various categories of hearer and the Holy Spirit's work in their lives
(6 lessons)

Sin and Its Cure (1 and 2 Kings – Elijah and Elisha)
The nature of sin and its punishment, with God's remedy graphically presented (8 lessons)

The Saviour Comes and Begins His Work (Matthew's Gospel – Part I)
A chronological account of the life and teaching of the Lord highlighting His attributes and saving purpose (12 lessons)

Lessons for Life 4 (lessons 139-184)

The Word of God (The Division of the Kingdom to the Exile)
The Bible authenticated in history and in transformed lives (11 lessons)

The Life, Death and Resurrection of the Lord Jesus Christ
(Matthew's Gospel – Part II)
Continuing the chronological account of the life and teaching of the Lord
(10 lessons)

Character Studies from Daniel and Nehemiah
The transforming work of grace and its dramatic results (9 lessons)

The Ten Commandments
The 'schoolmaster' to lead us to Christ and the way of safety and fulfilment
(11 lessons)

How God Fits Us for Heaven
The steps of salvation explained from Romans and other epistles and applied to young people today (5 lessons)

5. The *Lessons for Life* Bible Survey

ie: a different view from previous pages to show how Old and New Testaments are covered.

OLD TESTAMENT		NEW TESTAMENT	
Subjects	*Books*	*Subjects*	*Books*

Book 1

In the Beginning (Adam – Noah)	*Genesis (I)*	Miracles	*Mark (I)*
		Opposition to Christ	*Mark (II)*
God's Great Plans (Abraham – Joseph)	*Genesis (II)*	Paul	*Acts (I)*
		'I AM' Sayings	*John*

Book 2

The Pilgrimage from Sin's Slavery	*Exodus (I)*	Testimonies & Conversions	*Luke (I)*
Pictures of Salvation & Heaven	*Exodus (II) – Joshua*	Parables	*Luke (II)*
Judgement and Deliverance	*Joshua – 1 Samuel*		

Book 3

Great Differences: David & Solomon	*1 Sam – 2 Chron, Psalms*	Repentance & Faith	*Mark (III)*
		Early Church	*Acts (II)*
Sin and its Cure: Elijah & Elisha	*1 & 2 Kings*	Incarnation & Early Work of Christ	*Matthew (I)*

Book 4

The Word of God (later OT Kings)	*2 Kings & Chron, Amos – Jeremiah*	Death of Christ & Resurrection	*Matthew (II)*
Character Studies	*Daniel, Nehemiah*	Steps of Salvation	*Romans*
Ten Commandments	*Exodus 20*		

Section 5
THE TEACHING APPROACH

1. Qualities and Qualifications of Teachers

Teachers should be:–

- converted – with an ardent zeal to take the Gospel of their Saviour to others, particularly the young;

- awed – aware that they represent the Lord and are presenting His inspired, infallible Word;

- able to communicate – able to express in words care and concern from their heart;

- committed – ready to make sacrifices of time and effort for the sake of the precious souls entrusted to their care;

- conscientious – to prepare lessons, assemble visual aids, and attend to other duties such as visitation;

- willing – to be advised by, and to learn skills from, others, always being anxious to improve;

- patient – prepared 'to toil all the night and take nothing', or so it may appear. To be 'not weary in well doing', believing that, if they faint not, they will reap in due season *(Galatians 6.9)*.

Note that many of the best Sunday School teachers (and preachers) started in this work when very young. Spurgeon was in mid-teens, E. J. Poole-Connor was only 13. While these proved to be exceptionally gifted, their example will be an encouragement to serious young people to prepare themselves for the work.

2. The Duties of a Sunday School Teacher

(In addition to their teaching role described below) these include:–

- carefully keeping their own class register – a record for prayer and visitation;
- praying for each child – with concern and faith;
- visiting children's homes – to meet their parents, enter their world, understand their interests and their trials;
- listening to children – before and after class, at parties, outings, at weeknight meetings;
- watching for signs of spiritual life; also for their trials and worries. (For example, the process of applying for a place in a secondary school is a very big step for an eleven-year-old. Show an interest and encourage them);
- contacting children when absent, by telephone or through the person who collects them, or by a visit. If they are ill, visiting the hospital, taking a booklet to read or colour;
- contributing to the life and work of the Sunday School overall; volunteering help if they see a need arising which they could fulfil; sharing duties with others;
- remembering children after they leave the class, and following their natural and spiritual career. Continuing to pray, and waiting for good news, and especially news of conversion.

3. The Teaching Method

The art of whole-class teaching has been lost in many schools (especially junior age) but traditional teaching matches very well the biblical 'preaching' style, enthralling the children and touching their hearts. We firmly believe that the practice of a teacher addressing the whole class together, cannot be bettered. (Classes will preferably be small.) Nothing could be more appropriate for a message from the Creator, which is not up for discussion, is about serious matters, and should not be overly lightened by such things as play-acting. Inspired with a life-and-death message, many Christians discover they have a teaching gift, which they never knew about and which becomes a great blessing to young lives, and a great joy to themselves. Teaching the children the way to Heaven is one of the most precious and pleasurable experiences any Christian can have on earth. If only more believers would leave their 'nets' of everyday living and follow Christ in the business of fishing for souls!

4. The 'Five Pillars' of Sunday School Lessons

May a young child be saved? We believe most certainly that they can be. We therefore aim to teach the children five Bible doctrines necessary for salvation, always expressed very plainly. Contrary to the implied view of so much Sunday School material available today, these truths are probably grasped more easily by children with the blessing of the Holy Spirit, than by adults. Jesus said to adults, 'Except *ye* be converted, and become as little children, ye shall not enter into the kingdom of heaven' *(Matthew 18.3)* – not the other way round! Some or all of these doctrines should be included in every Sunday School lesson. They are the basis of the catechisms learned and recited by past generations of children. Examples are listed below of lessons which contain and particularly illustrate each salvation doctrine. Week by week we teach that in order to be saved and find the Lord, children, moved by the Spirit, can and must:

(1) *Believe in God Who created us, and all things*

The Bible begins with this foundation truth, which it is vital to stress in this atheistic age. Young children accept this as an obvious fact, but adults, brainwashed by evolution, find it more difficult to accept. This is not too difficult for even the youngest children, who readily see that they have a Maker to Whom they owe their gratitude, love and obedience.

(2) *Admit that they are sinners*

The Bible gives us many varied examples of sin and sinners and insists that sin must be acknowledged before the Lord may be known. Children are often in trouble, having to admit wrongdoing and demonstrate sorrow, whereas adults are reluctant to admit their fallen nature and their constant, wilful sins. Therefore we ought not to doubt a child's capacity to acknowledge their sin and to feel their great need of a Saviour, even in a society which brings up its young with contempt for moral values.

Example lessons from *Lessons for Life* which teach this doctrine: *Adam, Cain, Pharaoh, golden calf, Achan, Ahab, Naaman, Pharisees, lepers, Saul, the Philippian jailor.*

(3) *Repent of sin*

The Bible also gives many examples of the manner of true (and false) repentance. It warns that unforgiven sin will be judged and punished by God. Children know the difference between sincere and superficial repentance, and tears of true regret are not unknown to them. Adults are loath to lament over and apologise for their errors, and then to change their ways. Therefore we should urge children to leave behind their love of sin and ungodliness and seek forgiveness earnestly before the years of adult hardness set in. Moved by the Holy Spirit, they can accept that it would not be right to ask the Lord's forgiveness whilst still deliberately hanging on to those sins which made His death necessary. Tears of true repentance in a child are a precious sight to the Lord.

Example lessons from *Lessons for Life* which teach this doctrine: *Brazen serpent, Psalm 51, Manasseh, prodigal son, Zacchaeus, publican, Onesimus.*

(4) *Believe the Gospel*

The Bible teaches that there is no hope for anyone but in Christ and what He did for sinners on Calvary. Repentance, though good and necessary, can never itself save. Justification is by faith *alone*. Children will grasp this, for they live in constant dependence on others for their daily needs, and for instruction. Trusting another is a natural act for them, whereas adults are inclined to be self-sufficient and self-confident. It is the latter who prefer to earn their own acceptance by God. Therefore, the earlier we can urge children to seek and depend on the Saviour by grace alone, believing His invitations and promises, the better. Having found the Saviour they will be able to look to the future saying, 'Take myself, and I will be, ever, only, all for Thee.'

Example lessons from *Lessons for Life* which teach this doctrine: *Abraham, Joseph, Jonathan, Daniel, Nehemiah, wise men, centurion, dying thief, Cornelius, the Ephesian believers.*

(5) *Look to a 'better land'*

A Christian is one who has his treasure in Heaven, is waiting for the Saviour's return, and is living in the light of these glorious things. Children are always thinking, playing, planning, and learning for their future as grown-ups, but adults are wrapped up in the immediate concerns of their lives. Children are naturally oriented to look ahead. It is adults, not children, who refuse the Gospel because the present is too important. How vital it is to reach children with these soul-saving doctrines which, even from a natural standpoint, are well within their grasp.

Example lessons from *Lessons for Life* which teach this doctrine: *Canaan – a type, 'I am the Resurrection and the Life', Lazarus, Romans – glorified.*

5. A Checklist for Teachers Preparing a Lesson

(1) *Early in the week, identify the subject of the lesson* so you can begin to think it over, and look out for illustrations suitable for your class.

(2) *Read the Bible passage carefully:* the lesson notes are not a substitute for this.

(3) *Ensure the genuineness of your personal concern* for your class. Children will quickly spot an indifferent spirit.

(4) *Use the lesson books.* These 'summarise' the experience of many teachers over many years in presenting a Gospel message to children from Bible passages. Benefit from their experience.

(5) *Make notes.* Even if you are unable to refer to these during your lesson, the notes will help fix the essential form of the lesson in your mind so that you have liberty and fluency. List the points you plan to make under clear headings. Use colours to highlight particularly important points. If helpful, practise teaching the lesson to yourself.

(6) *Aim to make the lesson interesting.* In particular give thought to its introduction and conclusion. You need to capture the children's attention at first, and also to avoid a predictable, spiritual 'moral' at the close which children will recognise and ignore. These important parts of the lesson need to be fresh and compelling.

(7) *Cultivate the skill of varying the style* and timing of the spiritual application. Catch the children off guard and cause them to listen when they might not otherwise do so: the lesson notes give suggestions.

(8) *Prepare visual aids.* The *Lessons for Life* visual aids provide a wonderful and varied set of helps to the teaching of the lessons but teachers can add extra pictures or words. The following comments apply when teachers need to prepare their own visual aids. It is better to have a visual aid in which components can be added throughout the lesson, than a plain picture which catches their attention only once. Even hidden words have curiosity value. In a world of highly developed graphics, be sure that the work is not shoddy, bringing dishonour to the cause. Store past visual aids methodically for future use.

(9) *Examine your lesson outline* to check that it contains all or some of the five crucial doctrines or 'pillars' of salvation. It is better

to get one arrow of conviction, or one true glimpse of the Saviour's love, home to the children's hearts than to cover the entire plan of salvation in each lesson.

(10) *Ask the Lord's blessing* on every part of your labours, remembering His words: 'without me ye can do nothing' *(John 15.5).*

6. Hints for Teachers of Younger Classes

(1) *Never be condescending* or over-simple with little children. Often, as we have argued, they are more ready to understand spiritual matters than adults. (This is surely implied in the Saviour's words in *Matthew 18.1-6.*)

(2) Little children love to learn. *Don't waste their time* with nothing more than acting plays, colouring-in, or so-called Bible games. Few have parents with the time to read or talk to them at length, and often they will sit and listen to a straightforward lesson for longer than we would expect. Many teachers have discovered that even the youngest classes can follow a surprising amount of most *Lessons for Life* lessons. Don't be misled.

(3) When preparing a lesson, *imagine yourself in front of the class,* and so aim to keep their attention throughout. What a tragedy if the children were to find the lesson boring.

(4) *Get to know the children,* their homes and their interests so that you can speak to them naturally and seriously, and sometimes good-humouredly. The better you know the class, the easier it will become to extract the points from *Lessons for Life* lessons which apply to your age group.

(5) *Don't overtax the children.* It is no use continuing if they are not listening! The lesson is for the children – not the teacher. Make your notes but change tack if the children become restless. Use pictures, visual aids, etc to keep their attention. Be a little demonstrative – acting or living the part of some of the characters in the lesson if this comes naturally. Show, even in your face, your

concern for their souls, especially as you tell them about your wonderful Saviour, the sins that hurt Him, His dying love, etc.

(6) *Read for yourself* some of the traditional children's hymns and books (from days when large numbers of children were converted) to see how their writers encapsulated the Gospel in words for the youngest child along with a heartfelt response. For example, Fanny Crosby wrote many short, four-line verses – so simple yet so full of soul-saving truths, and far more consistent with reformed truths than many of the choruses in vogue today.

(7) Remember that your lessons given to the youngest classes are *building blocks for the future.* Don't be disappointed if you don't cover all the ground you intended. We trust the children will still be attending for years to come and that the next teacher will be able to build on the foundation laid in earlier years. Sometimes just one or two main points will be sufficient.

(8) *Use questions* to secure the children's attention at the start of a lesson, or if their minds are wandering, but *don't* allow these to interrupt your flow. (Don't allow one child to disrupt the class by asking you questions – often unconnected with the subject – in the middle of the lesson.) Revise last week's lesson. Repeat the main points frequently and simply. Little children love repetition and they like to show how much they have learned by answering questions. A short, pointed question (eg: 'Are you/we proud like the Pharisee? Have you ever asked the Lord to forgive you?') may be all that you need to apply the Gospel to their hearts.

(9) Young children respond well to the simplest of *incentive schemes.* A star on the chart or a Bible-text to colour, or a word of praise in front of the class inspires marked improvement in most cases.

(10) Little children find it *difficult to draw analogies.* Surprisingly perhaps, parables are more difficult for them than straightforward lessons. They confuse the story and its meaning. If we say the

shepherd is a picture of the Lord Jesus, they are likely to think that Jesus' work was out in the hills caring for the sheep! If we compare sinners with the prodigal in the pigsty, they are likely to imagine themselves literally wallowing in the mud!

Avoid drawing step-by-step parallels which give a meaning to every item in the parable. Better to relate the parable, and then tell the children quite separately the truths it illustrates. The value of the parable for these young ones is that, if told properly, it will arouse all the feelings and emotions which we want to stir when we teach the spiritual facts. We give below an example from the case of the prodigal son.

7. An Example Lesson for Younger Children – from a Parable

This perfect evangelistic parable taught by the Saviour provides a pattern for many lessons to children. The characters and events may vary, but the basic truths remain the same. Note the five 'pillars' in this parable of the prodigal son, taken from *Lessons for Life 2*. (This extract is the method recommended for very young children, and teachers of older classes should read the alternative approach suggested and recommended for them which follows this method in *Lessons for Life 2*.)

Text: *Luke 15.11-24*

Aim: To follow step by step the Saviour's portrayal of sinful rebellion, and His description of a true conversion.

Lesson Outline – For Younger Children

Relate the *whole* parable (without interruption for application) as vividly as possible, aiming to achieve the following:–

(a) *Appreciation* of the kind, good and generous character of the father. (Pillar 1.)

(b) *Horror* and *disgust* at the behaviour of his younger son who selfishly demanded his share of the father's will, went as far away as possible and squandered it on himself. Help the children to see what a callous and greedy person the son was. (Pillar 2.)

(c) *Pity* for the prodigal when events caught up with him and he found himself reduced to such squalor.

(d) *Relief* and *approval* when at last the son came to his senses and made his way home in shame, hoping that his father would accept him as a servant. (Pillar 3.)

(e) *Amazement* that the father, instead of being angry, was not only prepared to take him in, but rejoiced at his safe return, and gave him a dignified place in his household. (Pillars 4 and 5.)

Application. Proceed to explain the parallel Gospel facts, the hearts and concerns of the children having been awakened by the parable.

(a) Speak of the Lord God Who made this world, and gave every good and perfect thing in it. As you speak the children should begin to feel *appreciation* of the Lord's goodness. (Pillar 1.)

(b) Speak then of how boys and girls (and grown-ups) want to forget all about God, keep away from His house, give no thanks to Him for all His gifts, and have nothing to do with Him in their lives. Describe how lots of people use God's gifts just to please themselves (eg: food to be greedy with, etc). Help the children to view this attitude and behaviour with *horror* and *disgust.* (Pillar 2.)

(c) Tell the children where a godless, selfish life leads. Describe how people who live without God are nearly always unhappy, especially when life becomes hard and difficult. Draw out the children's *pity* for the unbeliever in these tragic circumstances. Point out that we are all in this sad state before we return to our heavenly Father.

(d) Ask them what is the best thing to do when we realise that we have sinned against God, and are a long way from Him. Encourage a sense of *relief* as you tell them that it is possible to pray to God, and to tell Him how sinful and wrong we have been. God wants us to ask for His forgiveness and to humbly offer to serve Him throughout life. (Pillar 3.)

(e) Explain that God, instead of sending us away from His presence for ever, sent the Saviour to die for us, and not only welcomes us back, but forgives us and makes us members of His own family. Speak of this with a due sense of *amazement*, and ask the children if they have ever prayed to God with shame and sorrow, and asked for His forgiveness. Urge them to do so, and to live close to Him for the rest of their days. (Pillars 4 and 5.)

8. Keeping Discipline in a Class

This is a universal, age-old problem in teaching. The best prepared lesson is worth nothing if children are not listening. Skills of discipline will yield lasting fruit, for order achieved in one group or generation of children will set the pattern for the next, and the reverent atmosphere in Sunday School will shape the children's concept of the Lord Himself and their attitude towards Him. Here are some points of advice –

Be resolute. Demand, as it were, a hearing. You speak for the Lord, not yourself. If the children give you five minutes of undivided attention to start with, you should be able to maintain their interest with a well-prepared, vital lesson. So don't begin the lesson until they are quiet and ready to listen.

Be a little firm and 'fierce' to begin with, so that they respect you. You can always become more friendly later. Lay down some rules for class behaviour (for example, 'No talking while I'm speaking') but these must be practical. Don't make threats you cannot or will not keep.

Supervise seating arrangements with care. Parting two chatterboxes will save a lot of trouble later. Reward good behaviour – eg: allow last week's best-behaved class member to have first choice of a seat this week.

Send out 'impossibles'. Don't allow one bad child to disturb the whole class persistently. Department leaders should make provision for children sent out of class. Some need personal supervision and encouragement, while a few may have to be 'rested' from Sunday School attendance for several weeks. It is a Gospel message in itself to make it clear that in the Lord's house rude, lawless behaviour is unacceptable.

Keep eye contact with the children. Don't bury your head in notes, or speak to the opposite wall. Look at the children! You are trying to *persuade* them. If you are losing their attention and interest, change tack by introducing a captivating illustration or anecdote. Have a store of these reserved for such emergencies.

Remember, 'Prevention is better than cure'. Aim to prevent trouble before it happens. Fear problems, so that you make every effort to avoid them coming about in the first place. Be punctual and fully prepared. If you give the children time to get restless, you start at a disadvantage. During the preliminary worship of the department, as you sit with your class, be sensitive to mischief. Listen for fidgeting during the prayer time: a tap on the shoulder will often put a halt to growing disruption. Cooperate with the department leader. For example, don't chat to an individual child after the bell has been rung.

Use incentive schemes. Star charts, text tokens, prizes and other reward schemes are much appreciated by children, but keep to the Sunday School guidelines. If one teacher awards more valuable prizes, children in other classes will regard this as unfair. If text tokens are awarded throughout the Sunday School, keep to the agreed number.

Test yourself. Ask: 'If I were a ten-year-old, would I want to miss a special television programme or football match in order to listen to my Sunday School teacher?' If children honour us with their attendance, when other alluring possibilities tempt them, do we not owe it to them to prepare our lessons well?

Emphasise the element of surprise. The Lord Jesus was never boring. His teachings always contained an element of surprise. Let Him be your example. Children will be enthralled as the characters in His parables who they would expect to be the 'goodies' (eg: the Levite, the rich man, the elder brother) turn out to be the 'baddies'.

(See Appendix 3 for serious breaches of discipline and the rules on how to handle them.)

9. The Seven 'Keeps' of a Sunday School Teacher

(1) *Keep a diary* – with notes of forthcoming Sunday School events. It undermines the work when teachers are constantly caught out, fail to contribute to the spirit of anticipation before events, or plan an absence at the vital time.

(2) *Keep notes* of your lessons with comments. Soon after the lesson, note what went well and how you could improve the explanation. By the time you come to present the same lesson again in four years' time, you will have forgotten, and the note will be precious.

(3) *Keep your register* – vital for prayer, visitation and as an official record of attendance when assessing prizewinners.

(4) *Keep time* – punctuality prevents all kinds of problems before they arise, not only indiscipline, but potentially dangerous situations with children milling around unattended.

(5) *Keep up your own attendance at ministry* on Sundays and midweek Bible studies, and keep up the habit of reading helpful books, so that your spiritual fervour is maintained, and your lessons stay fresh.

(6) *Keep praying* – no teaching technique will replace genuine, loving concern for the children's salvation, and they will sense and respond to this. Plead often with the Lord to bring them into His fold.

(7) *Keep on* – 'Let us not be weary in well doing: for in due season we shall reap, if we faint not' *(Galatians 6.9)*.

10. A Short, Basic Reading List for Teachers

(1) The Bible – other books are never a substitute, however good. Read it, love it, learn it, test your knowledge and attend ministry (a notebook will be helpful, especially for illustrations and arguments heard during evangelistic sermons).

(2) A confession of faith – summarising and proving the doctrines of the faith (eg: *Baptist Confession of Faith, 1689*).

(3) A systematic theology – eg: *Body of Divinity*, Thomas Watson, with its many fascinating illustrations of divine themes.

(4) *The Soul Winner*, C. H. Spurgeon – particularly the chapter on 'How to Raise the Dead', which was addressed to Sunday School teachers.

(5) *Sketches from Church History*, S. M. Houghton – to give a quick and illustrated review of the work of the Gospel from New Testament days.

(6) *Many Infallible Proofs*, Henry M. Morris – a wide-ranging book of apologetics, challenging the atheistic, evolutionary propaganda with which our children are bombarded.

(7) Biographies – Sunday School lessons will come to life if the teachers are keen readers. Wonderful life-stories will inspire and encourage in weary days. C. H. Spurgeon, a great lover of children and Sunday Schools, would be a good start.

(8) *The Necessity of Sunday Schools*, Peter Masters & Malcolm H. Watts – a clarion call for the unique effectiveness of *evangelistic* Sunday Schools operated on as large a scale as possible. Stimulation and encouragement is here in abundance, together with counsel and help for workers.

(9) *Children's Devotions for Morning and Evening*, Frances Ridley Havergal (revised 2005) – this book provides a wonderful

demonstration for teachers, despite its Victorian language, showing them how the greatest doctrines can be explained simply and feelingfully to the youngest child.

The *Read for the Lord* list of books, available from the Tabernacle Bookshop, is particularly helpful in establishing believers in all the vital doctrines of the faith and introducing them to a range of topics, along with biographical and apologetic books. Sunday School teachers who devote time to reading will find these books invaluable for stimulation.

Section 6
LEADING A DEPARTMENT

1. The Special Role of Department Leaders
2. The Main Responsibilities of Leaders
3. The Order of Service – a Suggested Programme
4. Leading in Prayer – Some Guidelines
5. A Good Department Leader
6. Leaders' Instructions on Discipline and Child Protection

All leaders should have read the church's policy statement on discipline and child protection, and leaders' rules (Appendices 1-3).

1. The Special Role of Department Leaders

It is the leader's role to welcome newcomers and regulars into the Lord's house. For some it may be the only contact they will ever have with a living church and the Gospel. The leader has the privilege of leading a team of evangelists pointing young lives on to the highway which leads to the Celestial City. Their task is to ensure that the impressions the children receive and the memories they take with them are worthy of the Lord.

Maintaining harmony. Two rules for department leaders of Sunday Schools, Bible Classes and other children's meetings are necessary in order that a balance may be struck between having liberty for initiatives, and not proceeding as an autonomous department drifting away from the oversight of the church.

Firstly, innovations and new ideas are always welcome but before implementing entirely new ideas, leaders must consult the Sunday School coordinator or the pastor. These may see problems relating to the School or the church at large, not spotted by the leader of the department.

Secondly, all speakers, helpers and other appointments must be agreed with the pastor *before* they are approached. The appointment might be quite inappropriate for reasons known only to him, and hard feelings may be caused if a person already asked has to be subsequently declined (see Appendix 1).

2. The Main Responsibilities of Leaders

(1) *General help to new staff members*

* Ensure all teachers are given a copy of the Church Policy, and Discipline and Child Protection Rules (see Appendices 1 and 3).
* Welcome new teachers to their department, giving them support and help in their early lessons. If appropriate, arrange for them to 'sit in' with an experienced teacher before starting with their own class.
* Give practical advice on discipline, the importance of punctuality and preparation in preventing problems; the department's ways of rewarding good behaviour and discouraging bad; where to send children who create a disturbance in class, etc.
* Outline procedures for obtaining, using and returning visual aids, visitation of class members, text token rules, etc.

(2) *Communication.* To ensure that every department continues to work harmoniously and efficiently, it is vital that leaders communicate with the coordinator or pastor, and other members of the team. Not only should they raise staffing needs (which must be advised in good time) and general problems, but provide a picture of how things are going.

(3) *Response to attendance figures each week.* When numbers fall, check that absentees are being visited and encourage prayer for the Lord's help. Ensure that incentive schemes are working well.

(4) *Care for the children in their department.* Know their names; pray for individuals whose interest, or lack of interest, arouses attention and notice their attendance or absence. Leaders are to be 'under-shepherds' to their flock of 'lambs'. They need to visit some

of the children's homes to get an insight into the children's surroundings and needs. Leaders should see that the children's work is represented in the church prayer meeting.

(5) *General presentation of their department.* This includes the standard of visual aids, the smartness of hymn and chorus sheets, the general brightness of the hall or room, and the tidiness of the cupboards used by their department. Help can be obtained from artistic members. While the basic programme will remain stable, the various items and presentations should *always have a new look.* It is easy to get into a rut. Plan variations on the same theme (novelties in the eyes of the children), eg: a new hymn to learn for the anniversary; a new poster to advertise the outing; new incentives for bringing a friend, and also for well-kept and completed Bible Learning Course leaflets. Holiday periods are a good time to look forward and plan a new and exciting term ahead.

(6) *Maintenance of good timekeeping.* Many problems start with failures in *punctuality* and leaders set the standard. Always start Sunday School on time even if some children are late. If you delay on one week it will only signal to latecomers that punctuality is unimportant and the problem will snowball. Careful preparation is key to the smooth running of the department. Early planning and provision of necessary materials is important. Leaders must have everything ready and be present in the hall well before the meeting starts. Timekeeping includes attention to the following:

- liaison with the person organising the transport of children;
- oversight of the layout of the room or hall (furniture and presentation);
- liaison with pianists, providing them with a music book of the tunes used. Each week give them a duplicate 'order of service' so that they have all the tunes ready before Sunday School begins.

(7) *Supervision of unruly children,* including the instruction of the department 'policemen', who should be prepared with an alterna-

tive to the weekly lesson (eg: a Bible reading with questions to answer) for children sent out of the class by their teacher. Often such children are seeking attention (and affection). Having alternative work for them to do means they do not escape a lesson but are receiving some individual care. The 'policeman' will give them encouragement to behave in class the following week.

After all efforts to reform them have failed, it is the leader's responsibility after consultation with the coordinator and teacher to 'rest' a persistently unruly child for a period. Wherever possible the leader should visit the home and explain the problem to the parent. (This will often throw new light on the root problem.) Children who constantly spoil the atmosphere and distract others *must* be rested, otherwise lesson times will be undermined for all and the good name of the Sunday School put at risk. Never ignore such situations. It is necessary (see Appendix 2) to keep a written record of any incidents of serious bad behaviour, so that should there be further enquiry the facts are to hand.

(8) *Organisation of special occasions* – anniversaries, prizegivings, Christmas services and open schools at New Year, Easter and during the summer. Most departments have recorded lists of arrangements to be made and experiences of past occasions. Leaders need to think a term ahead. (See Section 8 for details.) Department leaders must ensure the provision of letters or cards of invitation for special occasions in good time for teachers to distribute, so that children can be encouraged to attend.

(9) *Welcome of new children*
- Meet the new children each week and welcome them, learning their names if possible. Appoint, if necessary, a new-children's teacher to introduce them to Sunday School, explain the text-token system, and the possibility of attending weeknight activities. Make sure all new children are entered in the register.
- Ensure they receive a home visit during the following week from

their teacher or another worker who should introduce themselves to parents and welcome the child. If a visit is not possible, a phone call will be better than nothing.

- Check with the collector that they will call for the child the following week. It is a great failing if parents agree for the child to come, have them ready on the day and then no one calls to collect them.

(10) *Allocation of children to classes* at the beginning of the Sunday School year. The leader, knowing the teachers of the department and bearing in mind their preferred option, must decide which teacher will take which class. Early consultations with the teachers, and checking lists with the coordinator, will make for a happy, cooperative team. Once the decisions have been made, the registers can be prepared.

(11) *Keeping of a 'year-by-year' folder.* Many Sunday School events are held only once a year, and it is easy to forget how things went last time – the good points and the disasters. It is enormously beneficial if, within a day or two of the event, the leader jots down comments on the way things went, so that in future years faults are not repeated and improvements can be made. This procedure has an added benefit. If members of staff fail in some way, they need not be corrected immediately after the event at which they may have worked very hard, but the necessary improvement can be discussed with the benefit of hindsight when the item comes round next time.

(12) *Informing of financial procedures.* Teachers may wish to claim for expenses incurred, and leaders should explain the system – preferably via a Sunday School treasurer.

(13) *Prohibition of handling.* It is vital that department leaders ensure that children are not physically handled (except to separate fighting children – see Discipline and Child Protection Rules, Appendix 3). If a child is behaving in such a way as to provoke anger, the leader must withdraw the child and arrange for him or

her to be taken home immediately, if possible. Inform the parents of the problem and suggest that the child is 'rested' for a few weeks, until it is clear that his or her behaviour has improved. Often parents are having trouble with the child's behaviour at day school also and are glad to discuss the problem with a kindly Sunday School teacher.

3. The Order of Service – a Suggested Programme

Children appreciate a predictable, secure order in Sunday School. They also respond to novelty and interest-arousing items within this basic framework. One item should follow another quickly so that children are not given the opportunity to get restless.

It is important to always start punctually. The following plan has been considered with care and found helpful:–

(1) A form of *introduction*, eg: 'Good afternoon, children,' 'Welcome to Sunday School,' or 'Let us pray.'

(2) Sunday School *choruses or single hymn verses* (allowing latecomers to enter without causing disruption). Children love to be chosen to hold up the chorus sheet.

(3) *Bible reading* – a portion of the day's lesson chapter. Usually not longer than ten verses is the wisest course. The reading should be allocated in advance to a teacher with a loud, clear voice. Asking children to join in reading some verses helps them follow closely.

(4) *Prayer* (keep entrance door closed while in progress) – short and earnest. Not only *for* children but on their behalf (see p 68).

(5) *Hymn* – the choice of appropriate choruses and hymns for use in the Sunday School is vital. The best ones teach the children clear doctrine and reverence for God, while giving a clear Gospel call. They should be appropriate to the age of the children without being trite. Children carry these in their memory throughout life and into old age, so it is particularly important that they teach the right attitude to the Lord and convey soul-saving truths. Many of those

available to us are wonderful examples of Gospel appeals clothed in simple yet worthy language (understandable to the youngest child), and coupled with memorable tunes.

[A list of helpful choruses and hymns for children in the following categories is available: beginners (under 5 years); infants (5-7 years); juniors (7-11 years). Packs of suitable choruses and hymns can be purchased from the Tabernacle Bookshop and may be photocopied for local use.]

Many of today's children are unused to singing hymns, but leaders can teach them and, once they are under way, they will enjoy singing. Ask the pianist to play through a new tune once or twice before the children attempt to sing. Point to the words as the music is played. Encourage them to think of the words, but do not explain them at great length as this can be counterproductive.

(6) An item of *memory work*, either a hymn or Scripture verse (which could be based on the Bible Learning Course leaflet verse for the week). This activity is particularly helpful and attractive for younger departments. Coloured words may be progressively removed from the board as children recite the words over again.

(7) *The special item* – a short, illustrated talk (quite different to the lesson in character), given by the leader to the entire department, which should be kept to five minutes at the most in main departments. Suggested topics are available.

(8) *The lesson quiz* – questions on the previous week's lesson. This will encourage teachers to keep to the lesson notes, and children to listen and remember. Four to six questions are usually sufficient and a brightly-coloured chart (depicting a score 'race' between classes) will encourage classes to compete in providing the answers.

(9) *The notices* – encouraging children to attend weeknight activities, and forthcoming special events, and to participate in memory work competitions, etc. Good notices help to give Sunday School a living, vibrant atmosphere. Never underestimate their importance.

(10) *The direction* of children (and teachers) speedily and in an orderly way to their appointed place for lesson time. (The lesson

time includes the taking of the teacher's register and a lesson of about twenty minutes.)

(11) *The closing minutes,* when the children return from their classes to their department to hear a heartfelt plea to their souls from the department leader, to sing a hymn or a verse, and to hear a closing prayer. Leaders will need to have a plan for the children's exit so that this is orderly. If children are to redeem text tokens for rewards these should be in place on a manned table or stall so as to avoid delays.

Note: Drivers of Sunday School vehicles must be ready to drive off as soon as the children arrive outside.

4. Leading in Prayer – Some Guidelines

Insist on reverent silence through the time of prayer. Even godless youngsters can learn to respect that while you are addressing Almighty God they must not distract anyone.

Prepare your thoughts beforehand and be utterly genuine.

Be brief – long prayers cannot be followed by most unconverted youngsters, whose concentration span is very short. (The Lord's pattern prayer is an example to us in this matter.) What a tragedy if children resign themselves to looking round the room, and signing to their friends, while the leader or teacher prays at great length! Remember that prayer is a living demonstration – it may be the first time a young person has heard a believer pray – and their own approach will be shaped.

Address your prayer to God the Father, eg: 'Our loving, heavenly Father, we come . . . '

Vary the items for prayer so as not to repeat a predictable list of petitions which will not sound genuine if repeated week after week. Events in the life of your class, your church, and news which concerns the young, can be brought briefly to the throne of grace.

Ask yourself – Am I praying for the children (eg: 'Please Lord, help the children to understand') or on behalf of the children ('Please help us to understand')? Then keep to one style or the other.

Consider those who are young believers and pray on their behalf too. It will be an encouragement to them if you pray that the Lord will protect and guide them, and bless their lives and witness to others. This type of prayer will give the unconverted a glimpse of the living, dependent relationship between the believer and his Lord – which could be theirs too.

In helping very young children who have no idea how to pray, it may be helpful at times for the teacher to lead them in a short, simple prayer which they repeat line after line. This will need to be prepared beforehand to avoid stumbling and to ensure each 'line' is of a suitable length. However, don't let it sound like a dry, liturgical prayer.

Don't fall into praying for good behaviour, careful listening, not talking or distracting one another, which children will suspect is more addressed to them than God. Better to speak directly to the children on these matters and to pray to God privately for His help.

Key elements of prayer – the following headings provide a framework when considering matters for prayer, but should not be followed rigidly:

- *Worship* – give praise to God for Who He is and for what He has done in creation and salvation. (This should provide much variety in content.)
- *Thanksgiving* – for earthly blessings (especially those appreciated by children and young people), and supremely for the Saviour and His love (again, thought should be given so that this does not become 'vain repetition').
- *Repentance* – in which real sorrow is expressed for sin, emphasising different aspects week by week. Mention some sins common to the young, but not so as to trivialise. Sins of the heart should be included.

- *Intercession* – for the young people and their salvation; also for help in teaching the Word. It may surprise them to hear the depth (but not the length) of your concern.
- *Requests* – down-to-earth requests for particular needs; for example, people who may be sick, and missionaries known to the children; also for greater faith and dedication for those who already belong to the Lord; and for help to avoid temptation in the coming week (though not in a self-righteous way).
- *Confidence* – expressing faith and certainty that the Lord will hear and answer according to His perfect will – for His is the kingdom, the power and the glory for ever.
- *Conclusion* – in accordance with Christ's command prayers should be offered in His name, for only through His work may our unworthy prayers be presented at the Father's throne.

5. A Good Department Leader

A good leader will be responsible for the department 'come wind, come weather'. For example, the leader needs to:
- think of putting heat on early when the weather is very cold;
- persevere with a difficult child (though not allowing him or her to distract others);
- notice things going wrong and take steps to put them right *before* real problems take over;
- keep the spiritual goals in view, to encourage those who are laden with the practical jobs;
- report back to the coordinator or pastor if staff fail to turn up or fall short of a worthy standard;
- notice if staff miss attendance at Sunday or weeknight ministry unnecessarily (those who would win souls need themselves to be fed and inspired);
- care for staff who are experiencing special difficulties and encourage them;

- set a standard in personal appearance for staff, striking a Christian balance of care and thought, without any hint of attention-seeking;
- be willing to stand in at short notice if others suddenly fall sick;
- be willing to fill the gap if staff happen to be away at the same time (early listing of holiday arrangements may prevent this necessity). It is worth remembering that many who operate Sunday Schools where new churches are being planted are not able to take holidays at all due to lack of helpers;
- think of new ideas which will commend the Gospel to the children, keep them coming and hold behaviour problems at bay. Leaders need always to be thinking of next term's lessons, charts and needs;
- notice those in needful circumstances, such as (a) a large family who will find it difficult to finance four or five children to the Sunday School outing; (b) children who show particular spiritual interest. Relate to them, ensuring that they have a Bible for daily reading at home;
- be sensitive to a multi-ethnic situation, for example ensuring wherever possible that those leading the meetings reflect the groups represented and that prizes and books awarded do not represent an entirely different ethnic culture from that of the recipient;
- ensure the security of the Sunday School premises, even when this means staying late or making an unscheduled visit to check all is well and doors are locked.

6. Leaders' Instructions on Discipline and Child Protection

The leaders of each department and meeting have a vital role in ensuring the implementation of the rules for discipline and child protection. Leaders must be constantly alert to possible problems and dangers and must take appropriate action *without delay* to prevent problems arising. A list of duties is shown in suggested rules in Appendix 2.

Section 7
COLLECTING THE CHILDREN

1. A Collection Scheme

As the Sunday School grows and it becomes possible to recruit and collect children from several areas or routes, it will be necessary to appoint a reliable and capable person to oversee the system of collection – a 'transport coordinator'. If parents have been promised that the Sunday School will provide transport to and fro it is vital that this is honoured. As we have noted, parents will be disappointed, even annoyed, if the expected caller fails to appear and their children are let down.

The transport coordinator will need to be familiar with the local area, its flats, houses and streets. He or she should be aware of places which house large numbers of families so he can suggest where a new recruiting campaign could be targeted when this is possible. There is a tendency for well-meaning workers to agree to collect children from widely spread areas distant from the church, perhaps through a personal connection or recommendation, but the transport coordinator may need to resist sending Sunday School collectors on long digressions. These greatly reduce the numbers which can be brought from nearer homes.

He should also liaise with the pastor or a church officer appointed to approve a list of willing drivers and collectors of 'walk-in' children. He will need to provide drivers and collectors with detailed, accurate information about the children to be collected (see 'route pack' suggestion below), and explain what is required in a friendly, encouraging manner.

If the church owns minibuses, the transport coordinator should liaise weekly with whoever is responsible for the maintenance of vehicles to check their availability so that he may make other arrangements for the collection of children if necessary. He should be available by phone or in person to receive notice from any driver or collector who is unable to operate on a particular route, and make arrangements for another approved person to stand in.

Once the transport coordinator has organised his team of drivers and collectors, and allocated each to a route where they collect their children, the provision of a 'route pack' will be very useful.

Route packs are best kept in small, stiff plastic wallets which fit easily into a pocket or handbag. Each route is numbered, and each route pack contains a list of names and addresses of children to be collected on that route, together with a small map showing the precise route and order of collection of the children (especially for the benefit of a stand-in collector). The pack also contains invitation cards for parents. In addition it should contain a supply of registration cards needed when recruiting new children so that, if others want to come, the collector can obtain the necessary details from parents quickly and accurately.

Collectors should obtain their packs from a central point each week and hand them in on their return so that the transport coordinator is kept abreast of the numbers collected week by week. He can then make adjustments in the system to make full use of the transport and personnel available.

Vehicles

Minibuses, owned by the church or by members, and as many cars and drivers as possible enable large numbers of children to be collected whose parents are unable or unwilling to bring them along and who do not allow them to make their way alone. It is a good policy not to buy expensive, new minibuses, partly because their mileage will be far too small to warrant newer vehicles, and partly so that the available money can secure as many as possible. Members may be able to carry out basic maintenance. The vehicles need to look reasonably smart, and should be clearly marked with the name of the Sunday School (perhaps by smart, printed cards fixed to the inside of side windows) so that parents can be reassured. Fares, obviously, must never be charged for Sunday School travel or outings (where church or private vehicles are used) as this incurs considerable penalties in terms of tax and insurance, and requires PCV driving licences. (Even if hired coaches are used for outings, charging is a bad idea!) Under current UK law drivers under 70 years of age can drive minibuses on behalf of a non-commercial body for social purposes, with up to 16 passenger seats provided the driver is a volunteer, that no charges are made, the driver is aged 21 or over, and has held a car licence for at least two years. Drivers aged 70 or over need to meet higher medical standards. (Details: DVLA Fact Sheet INF28 www.dvla.gov.uk/forms/pdf/inf28.pdf)

2. Guidelines for Collecting Children

All staff involved in collecting children *must* possess a copy of the church's policy on collection. Details will vary according to local circumstances, but the following is used at the Metropolitan Tabernacle Sunday School and is given as an example.

(1) *Purpose*

Pick-up teams have a vital role in Sunday School work. They provide a key means of communication between parents and teachers. The continued attendance of children may depend as much on their collector as on their teacher. Collectors must endeavour to build a happy relationship with all the families whose children they collect.

Children are entrusted to our care by their parents. We must therefore give constant attention to their safety and well-being. These guidelines, together with the Discipline and Child Protection Rules, are designed to assist, and must be observed if the church is to continue to have the privilege of many children at Sunday School.

(2) *Safety*

It is easy to see that all the spiritual objectives of the Sunday School could be dashed if children were to be hurt or lost. The following rules are therefore vital:–

- Never bring a child to Sunday School without the permission and knowledge of his or her parent(s), and without obtaining the details required on the registration cards (name, address, date of birth, telephone number, etc), even if this means delaying his or her attendance for a week, during which you can call for the necessary information. A dangerous situation could arise if we had a child at Sunday School who became ill and whose address we did not know.

- If a child who has been collected changes his mind and refuses to enter the vehicle or premises, be sure to return him home and explain the situation to his parents.

- Always be on time. Children left waiting (whether at the church or on streets and estates) are open to danger.

- The youngest children should always be delivered right to their classroom on arrival, and collected from there to go home.

- On returning home, ensure children get into their flats or houses: do not just drop them off and leave them to find their own way indoors.

- Be sensible about physical safety. Keep children in a group and away from traffic while waiting for cars or buses. Wait until vehicles are stationary before allowing children to cross in front of them. Keep careful control as children move between stationary vehicles at the church, before and after Sunday School. At all times watch out and be alert for dangerous situations. Once children are in a vehicle, it must not be left unattended. Check that seat belts are fastened, and doors are firmly closed.

• While travelling, do not allow playing with doors, leaning out of windows or rough games. If children persist after a warning, report the matter to the transport coordinator or the children's department leader urgently.

(3) *New Children*

Generally priority is given to areas closest to the church when recruiting, so that the maximum use of transport can be made. Always take new children with their completed registration cards to the New Children's Desk on arrival at Sunday School. (A separate desk is assumed for larger Schools.) Ensure that details are correctly processed (as described shortly) and recorded in your own route pack. If young, find out which department a child will be in, so that you know where to collect him/her at the close of Sunday School.

Too many new children (particularly of the same age) on one Sunday can disrupt the atmosphere and be counterproductive. It is better to aim at a few recruits each week.

(4) *Misbehaviour*

The Discipline and Child Protection Rules must be adhered to by all of our children's workers. These include the principle – 'Prevention is better than cure.' Many problems can be avoided if staff are punctual. Dangerous situations arise when children are left waiting. Be watchful and ready to avoid and divert potentially difficult behaviour (eg: seat unruly children separately in vehicles).

(5) *General*

• If you have to be away on a Sunday, advise the transport coordinator as soon as possible so that arrangements for a stand-in collector may be made in good time.

• Relay information about the children to their teachers. In the case of important or urgent information (eg: child seriously ill, family moving, dissatisfaction with Sunday School, discipline problems, etc), let the department leader know also. The name of each child's teacher or department contact name is contained inside each route pack.

- If children swear, insult staff, act abusively to other children or damage the vehicles (eg: seating), that behaviour must be referred to the department leader.

- If standing in for the regular collector and not known to parents, carry some form of ID, eg: a Sunday School invitation card.

- Members of the transport team must discuss cases of repeated non-attendance with teachers and not decide themselves, without reference, to stop calling for a child.

- Aim to fill each seat in your vehicle. If there are vacancies and you are on a recruiting route, it may be helpful to canvass other families from the area you already visit.

- Encourage each child to bring their Bible.

3. Recruitment Campaigns

The transport coordinator will be a key person in recruitment campaigns.

General. In order to keep the Sunday School growing, it is important to organise fresh recruitment drives from time to time – perhaps at a time when the young people of the church are available to help. In a larger Sunday School it is a good idea for a planning meeting to be held at which the transport coordinator, Sunday School coordinator, and registrar select an area for visitation and plan the campaign.

A supply of Sunday School literature will be needed for helpers to deliver (see p 27 for points for a Sunday School invitation letter). Details of children whose parents are willing for them to attend should be recorded on a Sunday School registration card, and collection arrangements made.

Annual Visitation. To ensure a good start to the new Sunday

School year it helps greatly if an attractive newsletter can be produced and delivered to all families currently on the roll just before the new year begins (whether in September or January). Children are interested to read what is planned for the new term – the subject of the term's Sunday School lessons and the topic of the weeknight meetings. Special Sunday School events may be listed such as the prizegiving or anniversary to which parents are also invited. This all gives the Sunday School a living image and provides visitors with a talking point at the doorstep. Usually the result is a large attendance and increased friendly relations between homes and the church.

Sunday School Card. A small but attractively presented card giving a summary of the details of the Sunday School, its timing, contact details and a little about its activities, for regular use in recruitment is very useful. It can be made available to collectors, drivers and others doing district visitation as a means of giving information about the children's work. It can also serve as an 'ID' card particularly for those collecting children for meetings.

4. The Role of Registrar

It is essential that an accurate record be kept of all children who attend Sunday School. The person appointed as registrar should: (a) be able to keep a clear and accurate 'master' register; (b) have a heart-concern for the children (acting as a shepherd counting sheep in and out, and being aware of those who do not attend); (c) have a natural aptitude for remembering names and faces, so as to recognise the children on their list quickly. (In larger Sunday Schools it will be necessary to appoint a registrar for each department.)

The role in practical terms includes:

For the arrival of new children the registrar will ensure that a helper lists in a book their name, address, date of birth, telephone number and Sunday School collector. The collector should provide these details on a card. No child should be brought in without these details. In the event of accident or illness they are vital. The date should be noted also, as this may be needed in the years to come, as well as the name of the teacher to whose class the child is allocated.

At the beginning of the lesson pass a copy of these details to the teacher and add the name and address to the route pack (if these are kept) to remind the collector to call for them the following week, and encourage teacher and collector to work together to enhance the child's attendance in future.

On subsequent weeks the registration team at the entrance desk will record the child's attendance on the department register as they pass into Sunday School.

At the close of Sunday School the registrar should collect the attendance figures of each department and present these to the leaders, so that prayer and visitation schemes can be informed.

At regular intervals the registrar should provide register details to the department leader so that he may check that absentees are being visited. Low numbers can usually be traced closely to failure to visit. The registrar should be willing to help in the visiting of absentees.

Prior to prizegiving the registrar will need to provide an accurate record of each child's attendance over the past year so that prizes can be awarded fairly.

Prior to *recruitment campaigns* the registers will provide helpful information, indicating which areas are good 'fishing grounds' and which have been neglected up to the present.

At the *beginning of the Sunday School year* the registrar can provide an addressed envelope for every Sunday School family so that each can have literature (eg: a newsletter) delivered by a friendly teacher or collector. Those who have fallen by the wayside during the school holidays will be reminded to return for the new term. Thus the new year gets off to a good start, a crowd always attracting a crowd as far as children are concerned.

Section 8
THE SUNDAY SCHOOL YEAR

1. The Sunday School Anniversary

Purpose: A Sunday School anniversary is a special occasion when the whole School unites to mark the Lord's goodness over the past year. Parents and members of the congregation are invited to join the service of praise and to be given an insight into the nature and work of the School.

Events from the history of the Sunday School or church which fascinate the children can be recalled. Plans for the future year (eg: the destination of the Sunday School outing) can be unfolded.

Much will depend on the care and enthusiasm of the Sunday School leaders in planning and preparing the afternoon hour. The speaker will have a special opportunity to apply the Gospel message very directly to the children. Prayer that the occasion will mark the conversion of children, and make a deep impression upon parents, should be an item of great importance at the church prayer meeting.

Today's parents expect open days at the children's day schools. Anniversary, prizegiving and Christmas services provide a similar opportunity. Unchurched parents attend God's house and see the Lord's people in a natural, unintimidating setting.

Practical preparations for the Sunday School leader:

(1) Read the Sunday School 'year-by-year' folder to see if any improvements on the previous year's anniversary can be made.

(2) Early in the year fix the date. Avoid dates when large numbers of children or staff are likely to be absent, such as bank holiday weekends.

(3) Book a speaker (in good time, often months ahead). A visiting speaker is desirable if one is known and can be vouched for. It is not advisable to invite a speaker who does not seem to know how to bring the cross of Christ into his address.

(4) Arrange for a group of children to practise a special Bible reading in good time.

(5) Plan the programme early, so that hymns can be practised in advance and children can get to know anything special which is to happen. Arrange for hymnsheets to be made available. If the Sunday School is multi-ethnic it is important that all racial groups are represented on the platform party in some way, whether leading or reading Scripture, etc.

(6) Arrange for a member of regular staff to devise a quiz as an attractive item for the afternoon, with bright pictures of recent lessons. (Such a quiz will indicate to visitors that children have remembered recent lessons.) Ask six questions at the most for a large group, or children will get restless.

(7) Invitations of an attractive nature need to be designed, printed, photocopied and distributed in previous weeks. These should be given to children and church members (being left on entrance tables). In particular, obtain cooperation of collectors and teachers who can deliver these to families with warm, personal encouragement to attend. If not always successful, these at least provide an opportunity to relate to parents.

(8) Contact the speaker, asking about possible needs such as a visual aid stand, hospitality, transport, etc.

(9) Make arrangements for the afternoon's organisation. A printed plan will save time and worry, and help share the workload. This plan will provide for –

- *a pianist*, who has the music and is competent to play for a larger group, and who will have hymn music ready for playing during the entrance of children into the hall;
- *directions* (clearly printed on a board) for children and parents to go to the correct meeting hall, with a person to direct and welcome them as they arrive;
- *hymnsheets* to be printed and put in the right place;
- *display of visual aids*, children's work, weeknight-meeting topics, etc, to inform parents and to decorate the hall;
- *simple flower display*;
- *instructions* to be given to those who put out the chairs if this involves a different layout from usual;
- *appointment of a steward or stewards* to direct children and visitors to their seats, making them feel welcome (an unstewarded event involving children quickly becomes a noisy shambles);
- *Bible Learning Course leaflets* to be available for those who distribute these at close of meeting;
- a team of people to *tidy up*, and return artwork to its correct place after the meeting;
- someone to provide for *a visiting speaker's needs* (refreshments, etc), and to express the thanks of the Sunday School;
- a reminder to the church treasurer to provide for the *speaker's expenses* if appropriate;
- *the appointing* of a suitable person to shake hands and give a personal word of encouragement to parents who attend;
- *subsequent recording* of how the afternoon went, with ideas for improvements the following year, to be kept in the 'year-by-year' folder. Leaders themselves should thank the speaker warmly.

2. The Sunday School Prizegiving

Purpose: An annual Sunday School prizegiving service encourages children, parents and church members alike. Prizes are awarded, not for ability, but for attendance. In addition children can be given a further opportunity to win a prize by learning by heart the year's memory passage from the Bible. Parents and children look forward to this special occasion when each prizewinner hears their name read out and goes forward to receive their prize – a Christian book that will be treasured for years to come, and which acts as a reminder of Sunday School days.

Arrange for an artistically gifted member to print (by computer or in italic hand lettering) the year's memory verses. Copies may be fitted in picture frames for memory work prizes. Suitable frames, perhaps 5 inches x 3 inches, may be obtained in bulk at small expense. Children from the most godless homes will very often display these in their bedrooms – a touching sight.

Children who do not qualify for either of these prizes can be encouraged to start building up a good record for next year's prizegiving – and receive a small consolation gift as they leave (eg: a bookmark with a text, or a sweet).

The giving of prizes will occupy quite a large chunk of the afternoon programme, but a speaker will have time to give a short, well-aimed Gospel address to the gathered assembly. Otherwise the service may follow the same pattern as that on the anniversary Sunday.

Preparing for Prizegiving

(1) Book prizes. The following arrangements need to be made for the provision of prizes:–

Early in the year research suitable books for prizes at the right prices. Department leaders should show a selection to teachers so that they may choose books for their children who qualify for prizes.

Teachers will need guidance on the value of grades of prizes, which are – 1st class (say, for 75% attendance and higher), 2nd class (say, for 50% attendance and higher). A supply of coloured texts or colour-in books can make up the difference between one grade of prize and another. (The Tabernacle Bookshop can provide a list of reasonably priced books recommended for various age groups.)

Selection of prizewinners. At the close of the previous Sunday School year, registrars should make a list of children who qualify for prizes, check it with class teachers, and hand it to the department leaders who may think it wise, after seeing the list, to adjust the qualification, so as to be fair to all types of children.

Arrange for a person with good handwriting to write the names of prizewinners on appropriate labels in good time for prizegiving.

On prizegiving day, lay out the (clearly named) books on a table at the front of the hall. The registrar (who will be familiar with all the children) can hand these to the church member who has been chosen as the year's prizegiver (perhaps the pastor or a deacon, ideally with a kind, cheerful manner), to give the child a warm handshake and 'well done'. On this occasion it may well be appropriate for the School to clap, not for each individual giving of a prize, but for all prizewinners in each department.

(2) For memory work – select suitable verses from Scripture for children to memorise. Provide each child with words printed out in large type to take home and learn by heart. Lay the verses out to follow a pattern and so aid memorisation.

Start teaching memory verses each week in Sunday School early on. The rote method is very effective and provides a worthy item in the Sunday School programme for a period of six to eight weeks before the prizegiving. The weekly recitation by the whole department is quite affecting to listen to, and will help most children learn the verses almost without trying. Little children enjoy words written in different colours, gradually removed, until they know whole verses. Incentives along the way (eg: first child to be able to recite verses in class gets a small prize) will help.

If, in the case of a large Sunday School, there is not time to give out memory work prizes after the attendance prizes, or because the procedure is becoming boring, ask the children to collect them on their way out, but read out the names of those who have qualified to the School and allow a short burst of applause at the end of the reading of the list.

3. Open School in August, Easter and Christmas Holiday Weeks

Purpose: Open school enables children to keep the Lord's Day even in school holidays when teachers also have holidays. Individual class lessons are suspended and departments are taught as a whole. Sunday School attendance may be as large as ever, and the unusual format makes for an interesting change for the few weeks. It provides an opportunity to send out special invitation cards reminding parents and children that Sunday School does not close in the day-school holidays. Prior to the holiday weeks, leaders will need to make a roster of duties to be spread among teachers, allowing for their absences. Leaders, pianists, quiz-providers and speakers will be needed for each department.

Programme changes. Obviously, there are no classes – the lesson in each department being delivered by one of the more able and experienced teachers. This gives such teachers experience at teaching a larger group, while less experienced teachers have the opportunity to watch and learn. Other possible variations:

- Learn a new hymn.
- Have a 'quiz' (but not too many questions), with a large, bright scoreboard.

The special item/short talk should be omitted, otherwise children will have two talks in the same place in one afternoon, and the first speaker will steal attention from the second. Instead, children could learn verses from Scripture, or the leader could give brief news of church missionaries with a suitable map, photos, etc.

4. Hints on Speaking at Special Sunday School Occasions

The occasion provides a privileged opportunity to present the Gospel to a large audience of children with adults listening. Your aim – in dependence on the aid of the Holy Spirit – is to make this message the means of bringing a spiritual 'birthday' to many a child's soul.

Hints on preparation.

- Avoid subjects which are being taught currently in the Sunday School. If you are not a regular member of the team, visit the department on a previous week *to get a feel for the children,* their needs and level of understanding. Talk to the department leader.
- Spurgeon said, *'Our aim is conversion,'* so aim not just to get a good hearing but to confront the children with the call of the Saviour. Consider the 'Five Pillars' (on p 47) and how all or some can feature.
- *Use visual aids* to win and hold attention and to make points 'stick' in the mind. Only a very skilled speaker is likely to succeed without some visual help for children. But avoid visuals which take attention from matters of the heart. Even lesson headings, printed clearly and attractively can keep the children waiting and watching.
- *Repentance and faith – the balance.* It is important for modern children to realise that following Christ along the narrow road involves leaving the broad way. Repentance is important but never give the impression (as some children's speakers are prone to do) that repentance *earns* salvation. The death of the Lord Jesus on the cross of Calvary and a child's trust in Him is the

only way to conversion, so time and concern is needed to do this justice. *Galatians 6.14,* 'God forbid that I should glory, save in the cross of our Lord Jesus Christ' applies equally to messages given to children, as to adults. Sometimes a talk on a topic (eg: diseases of the heart) could be considered so as to make a change from the normal Sunday School lesson.

- Ask the leader *how long your message should last* and take care to keep to this. If you go over time, it may not only spoil the talk and lead to boredom, but it can also upset the complexities of getting children home safely and on time.
- *Avoid leaving the heart application* to a long, predictable 'lecture' at the close.
- *Avoid a merely emotional appeal.* Children can be very responsive, but giving them the impression that they can 'decide for Jesus' lightly can be damaging, causing them in later years to be cynical about Christian conversion.

Hints on presentation.

- *Smile as you begin to talk.* Think of the children and this will help you forget your own nervousness. Capture their attention at the beginning and then ask the Lord to help you keep their attention.
- *Speak up clearly.* A large hall will need amplification.
- *Have visual aids ready mounted* or arranged to display as quickly as needed.

5. The Sunday School Party

Purpose: To gather the children who regularly attend Sunday School and reward them in (say) midwinter with a happy afternoon with their 'Christian family', demonstrating that Christians can have fun and enjoyment without recourse to disco-style entertainment. It is also an opportunity for teachers to relate to their class members in a natural and friendly way.

Planning. The date of the party needs to be fixed well in advance, making sure it does not clash with another church event. Leaders will need to consider early items which have to be pre-booked such as a suitable video. It is most important that leaders have no other responsibilities during a party than overseeing events. If the leader is not available to observe and troubleshoot, real problems can arise. The leader's chief task will be to ensure that each group adheres to the timetable. With a large group of excitable children, the quality of coordination makes or mars the event. If, for example, a group of lively junior boys is kept waiting for tea by a group of beginners, the atmosphere can be harmed.

Invitations. A smart but cheerful, named invitation, given out at Sunday School on a previous week, and which children must show as they enter, will prevent 'gate-crashers'. Any children whose behaviour is so bad that they would destroy the happy atmosphere should not be invited.

Decorations. A few balloons, for example, can transform a schoolroom into a party hall; so decorations make all the difference but this should be done in moderation. Set a budget and give rules for where items can and cannot be stuck!

First aid. A doctor, nurse or first-aider should be available in case of accidents. Check that the first-aid cupboard is well-equipped.

Games. Avoid 'body-contact' and violent games which invite danger and unruliness. Have a clear leader for each group to organise the games session and who the children know is in charge. Games are over surprisingly quickly so have plenty prepared. Have all the equipment ready and laid out *before* the start. Have a whistle or other means of gaining attention. Before starting the games session, gather the children and explain the procedure, insisting that everyone responds to the whistle or bell.

Have some simple prizes available, either for individuals or for a team. A graphic team-competition chart on view from the start can be used to encourage good behaviour throughout the afternoon, especially with older, noisier groups. In order to gain a quiet period between games (when the next game can be described), award a prize for the first team to be seated in silence in its corner, after the signal is given. Boys tend to like physical games with plenty of (controlled) running about. Girls may prefer 'artistic' games. Games which involve periods of silence (eg: turning children into sleeping lions or statues when the bell rings) provide welcome moments of quiet.

Tea. Keep the meal simple but attractive; a few table decorations will help. Ask volunteers in the church to make decorated cakes. Begin the meal with a brief but heartfelt prayer of thanks – over the years children will learn to expect and respect this item of Christian life.

Entertainment. Start searching in good time to find suitable and not overlong videos. Prepare the room so the programme can begin immediately each group of children is assembled. Appoint a teacher to be in charge, to establish calm before the video begins. This person should have an item prepared should there be a technical hitch during the presentation.

Gift. A simple wrapped gift (possibly a sweet item) ends the party on a happy note. If thought of earlier in the year, toys or novelties at a bargain price may be spotted by an alert member of staff.

Parents. Parents will usually collect their youngsters from a party, and an opportunity to meet and break down barriers of shyness is thereby available. Provide them with refreshments and show some photos of previous Sunday School parties and events, along with a display of visual aids. This will provide an opportunity to talk about what the children are taught. Have some church literature and tracts available too. Invite them warmly to come to a Gospel service.

Tidying up. Many who help at the party will have their own young children to take home soon after it ends. Be sure to have a team (perhaps the young singles) to stay and clear up. Depute a responsible adult to check all is clean and secure before leaving.

Lessons to be learned. As with all events, make notes of the successes and problems. This will be invaluable for the following year.

6. The Sunday School Outing

Purpose: To take the children (some of whom may be underprivileged and not expecting a family holiday) out of town to the countryside or a place of interest for a happy day with their teachers and Christian friends. For many this will be an unforgettable experience, giving them a taste of the Lord's kindness both in the surroundings and the company. It provides teachers with an opportunity to relate to individual children, to demonstrate friendship, to listen to and share conversations through the day.

Planning. Early in the year appoint a responsible person to organise the outing and to research a *suitable venue* for the day. You will need a pleasant place, not too far away, without the attractions of, for example, a fairground, which will wholly absorb the children's attention, defeating the object of the exercise. You will need an area of grass where they can play games, possibly an adventure area, a place possibly where they can paddle and play in the sand, or a children's zoo (for the beginners' department), a model railway on which they can take a ride, or other wholesome pursuits. Check that there are sufficient toilets for your party size. Check that the venue is a safe place – where children cannot easily wander too far away and get lost.

Advance preparations. Check that the venue is available for a party booking on the date you require, and discuss your needs with the authority involved. They may lay on extra staff for safety. Book transport if you need an outside firm.

Inform the church officer who keeps the church diary so that the date can be reserved by all involved. Arrange for members not helping on the outing to provide tea for the children on their return.

Nearer the time. Write out a programme for the day, listing duties of various teachers and helpers, and the timing of all events.

Remember the following items and personnel:

- First aid, and a trained person able to administer this.
- Games equipment and organiser (skipping ropes, tug-of-war rope, bats, balls, whistles, sacks, prizes, etc).
- Drinks, if these can be taken (often they are very expensive on site).
- Lost property custodian.
- **Most important and helpful – coloured ribbons about 6 inches long to be tied on the wrists of all teachers and children so that your party can be quickly identified in a large crowd. (Children should be warned not to go off with anyone not wearing such a ribbon.)**
- Make an alternative plan in the event of the weather being unsuitable for a full day's outing. A video may need to be on hand should the party have to return early.

Give out invitations several weeks before the outing listing the day's activities with a portion for parents to sign giving permission for their children to go, and to notify of any allergies or relevant medical conditions. The invitation will state the cost if any (but note that there should be no fare charged if church vehicles are used, for reasons stated earlier). Children should return their consent forms on the Sundays prior to the outing, and certainly by the morning of the outing. The Sunday School should never take a child to such an outing without their parent's written permission. A registrar who keeps a list of names, should allocate each child to a teacher to ensure that each child is watched throughout the day.

On a weekday before the outing a briefing session should be held for teachers and helpers so that the organiser can give details of the day's arrangements. It is wise to impress upon staff that it is their responsibility to watch out for the children in their care as well as to enjoy the day getting to know the children. It may be necessary to remind them that it would be a disaster for the Sunday School if a child were to be lost or injured.

The person organising the day will need to check that the transport company knows where to pick up the group, and the best and shortest route to the venue.

On the day the organiser and team will need to start early, gathering equipment, and arranging furniture before the children arrive at the church.

Someone should be appointed to list children on to particular vehicles on the way out and to check that the same children are on board before leaving the venue.

Hopefully the day will go according to the carefully laid plans and children, teachers and parents will have cause to thank the Lord that such a happy time has been enjoyed.

Soon after the event, record good and bad points about the day as with other activities so that further improvements may be made the following year.

7. A Note on Weeknight Meetings Throughout the Year

The Sunday School, operated as an outreach to all the children and young people of a neighbourhood, is the central focus of the church's ministry to the young, but in order that staff may get to know children better, and to encourage regular attendance, a weeknight meeting should be organised (in day-school term time).

A policy which has proved successful over many years, is to insist on Sunday attendance in order to qualify for weeknight meetings. Apart from encouraging Sunday attendance, this reduces the tendency of weeknight meetings to become 'clubs' and to drift into an independent life apart from the Sunday work. We would, therefore, discourage the use of a weeknight meeting as a bait or springboard to Sunday attendance.

In today's culture, some children have little close parental interest, and the dedication of weeknight meeting workers is a powerful witness to the love of the Saviour.

Format and activities. The weeknight meetings engage the interest and enthusiasm of children by a programme of games and activities. The tendency is often to make handicrafts and games over-elaborate, but today's children, brought up on electronic amusements, actually find simple board games, puzzles and cooking, along with table tennis and snooker, to be quite absorbing. Some churches have facilities for outdoor games, but many also have nearby park facilities which may be used or hired for children. An hour of activities followed by a half-hour devotional time is greatly enjoyed by most youngsters. For devotions, by the time the children are settled and an introductory prayer has been offered, the actual time for the talk is around 20 minutes.

Syllabus. The weeknight meeting needs to have its own syllabus, different in character from that of the Sunday School. *Lessons for Life* Term Topics provide notes for weeknight meetings which are based around a theme for each term. Subjects are presented in an exciting way. Christian history, apologetics, biography and creation science yield enthralling topics offering the young information they are often denied elsewhere. These talks, interspersed with testimonies of invited people and other items, are very popular.

Published topics include:

'Why Believe in God?' – answers to atheists.
Matters of Life and Death – details of Heaven (and hell) from the Bible.
The Bible, an Amazing Book – many facts to surprise.
The Bible and Medicine – with some missionary stories.
Prayer – viewed from many fascinating angles.
The War of the World Against the Word – exciting church history in disguise.

A number of other Term Topics are nearing publication, which readers may wish to enquire about. These will be:

Messages from Space – Gospel lessons from the sun, moon, stars, etc.

The Bible: Fact or Fiction? – Bible history vindicated by archaeological discoveries.

Sowing Gospel Seed Around the World – exciting stories of early missionaries.

Things Wise and Wonderful – Bible lessons from familiar objects.

The Bible and Science – great scientists who were believers, and the creation/evolution debate.

The Holy War – weekly readings from John Bunyan's book (revised for modern readers by Thelma H. Jenkins) with artwork to bring the places and characters to life.

A Closing Word

It is hoped that this book will have been of practical help and encouragement to all who desire to reach the needy, rising generation with the Gospel of our Saviour. Some may be gathering a few children in their home or in a small building, others are struggling to cope with scores or hundreds. The promise of the Lord that His Word will not return to Him empty *(Isaiah 55.11)* proves a great incentive to continue through days of patient toil.

Slowly and surely the satisfaction of watching God's Word taking effect in the lives and behaviour of young children confirms its truthfulness. In days of irreligion and apathy in the adult population, it is extremely touching to witness numbers of children gathered together, and to see the Lord still preparing His praise out of the mouths of infants *(Matthew 21.16)*.

Some are privileged to watch their church fellowship grow as converted children, and their parents who once were hostile unbelievers, join the ranks of those who leave the world's side and follow Christ. Others will almost be moved to tears as they hear how the Holy Spirit has used memories of Sunday School days to pierce the heart and bring back to the fold, those who have wandered far away in adulthood. It is at such moments that the Lord's promise is gloriously authenticated even before eternity – 'He that goeth forth and weepeth, bearing precious seed, shall doubtless come again with rejoicing, bringing his sheaves with him' *(Psalm 126.6)*.

James Montgomery, a great promoter of Sunday Schools penned the grand old hymn which may serve as a wonderful motto for Sunday School staffs:–

> *Sow in the morn your seed,*
> *At eve hold not your hand;*
> *To fear and doubting give no heed,*
> *Broadcast it o'er the land.*
>
> *We know not which may thrive,*
> *The late or early sown;*
> *Grace keeps the precious seed alive*
> *When and wherever strown.*
>
> *And duly shall appear,*
> *In living beauty, strength,*
> *The tender blade, the stalk, the ear,*
> *And the full corn at length.*
>
> *We cannot toil in vain;*
> *Cold, heat, and moist, and dry*
> *Shall foster and mature the grain*
> *For garners in the sky.*
>
> *Then, when the glorious end,*
> *The Day of God is come,*
> *The angel reapers shall descend,*
> *And Heaven cry, 'Harvest home.'*

Introduction to Appendices 1 to 3
Discipline and Child Protection Policies

The following Appendices are based on the Discipline and Child Protection documents in use at the Metropolitan Tabernacle in 2005. These follow the current guidance of official bodies such as the London Child Protection Committee who have taken account of the provisions of the Children Act 1989 and the Protection of Children Act 1999. The approach taken is appropriate in England and Wales but readers in Scotland and other countries will need to ensure compliance with local laws and statutory regulations.

Our approach has been to ensure compliance with the law through procedures which are workable and can be maintained without imposing excessive demands on church workers. By implementing such procedures we demonstrate that we are a trustworthy organisation which parents and their children can rely on, knowing that staff have been carefully selected and trained, and that all staff have been briefed on these rules.

The four documents currently in use at the Metropolitan Tabernacle are:–

Church Policy Statement – agreed by the elders and deacons and displayed on church notice boards (Appendix 1).

Leaders' Duties in Relation to Discipline and Child Protection – all leaders of departments are to work to these duties which place on them important responsibilities for oversight of these matters within their own departments (Appendix 2).

Discipline and Child Protection Rules for All Sunday School Workers – every person who has any role in the church's children's work must receive and comply with these rules (Appendix 3).

Guidelines for Collecting Children – for all drivers and collectors of children to ensure safety during collection and take-home. (See pages 75-78.)

Appendix 1
Church Policy Statement

This is an example of a Church Policy Statement, such a document should be supplied to all involved in the work.

The Tabernacle seeks to reach as many children and young people as possible with the Gospel of Jesus Christ. This mission is largely expressed through the work of Sunday Schools, Bible Classes and weeknight meetings for all ages. Outings, parties and other special occasions are also held.

Throughout the operation of these meetings, and during the collection and transporting of children, the safety, protection and welfare of the children is the first priority.

The implementation of the church's policy is through the following procedures:

(1) All aspects of the policy, procedures and operation of the children's work are under the authority of the pastor, supported by the Elders' and Deacons' Court of the church. Day-to-day operation of the children's work is managed by the Sunday School coordinator, consulting the pastor, the coordinator being appointed by the Elders' and Deacons' Court.

(2) All appointments of children's meeting staff will be made by the pastor in conjunction with the Sunday School coordinator. No unofficial appointments will be allowed. No person with a history involving child-related offences will be allowed to undertake any role associated with the children's work of the church, nor be present as an observer.

(3) All leaders, teachers, and other responsible appointments will be members of the Tabernacle who have shown themselves to be trustworthy and faithful in all aspects of their lives.*

(4) Non-leading helpers may include people who are not mem-

bers of the Tabernacle. These must be approved by the pastor and will normally be members of other churches of like beliefs currently worshipping with us, and will be very well known to us as responsible and trustworthy Christian adults. They will always work under the supervision of Tabernacle members.

(5) Any member of staff or helper who manifests any irresponsible behaviour or loss of self-control in connection with the children, will be immediately suspended from his or ner child-related duties. Following investigation by the pastor and elders it may be deemed necessary to confirm the suspension as permanent.

(6) The 'Leaders' Duties in Relation to Discipline and Child Protection' will be given to each department or meeting leader.

(7) All leaders will be briefed on the Tabernacle's policy and related procedures by the Sunday School coordinator or one of the elders.

(8) All staff must be given the 'Discipline and Child Protection Rules', and be briefed on these by their department or meeting leader.

(9) A record will be kept of those briefed, and when. This will be reviewed every autumn.

(10) All new teachers must undergo a training course, which will include the 'Discipline and Child Protection Rules'.

(11) A logbook will be available for each Sunday School site to record any accidents or incidents. Entries should be made by the leader on the same day as the occurrence.

(12) Drivers of Tabernacle vehicles or private cars used for transporting children will be currently active drivers who are at least 25

---

*Increasing numbers of churches are vetting their Sunday School workers by 'Disclosure' checking with the Criminal Records Bureau. Although this is not a legal necessity, it is recommended by the Home Office, and churches are able to apply for checks for a fee or via a recognised 'umbrella' organisation. Such checks should surely be considered for new workers whose background is not well known to you, if not on a regular basis. (See www.crb.gov.uk)

years of age (for Tabernacle vehicles) or 21 years of age (for private vehicles), having held a full driving licence for at least 2 years and having no motoring convictions. All private vehicles used will be approved by a person appointed by the Elders' and Deacons' Court and must be insured with passenger liability cover. Drivers of church minibuses will be qualified in accordance with current legislation and listed as Approved Drivers with the motor insurance company of the Tabernacle.

(13) The activities to be undertaken on all children's outings, camps or other special occasions are to be fully agreed in detail with the coordinator and with an officer appointed for this purpose by the Elders' and Deacons' Court. The full implementation of all our Discipline and Child Protection documents is mandatory on all such occasions.

(14) The Sunday School coordinator will act as the contact for all discipline and child protection issues. He or she will quickly gather the available facts concerning any reports of suspected abuse of children and of any serious incidents involving Tabernacle workers. He or she will pass these to the pastor and elders, who will decide on appropriate action.

(15) The pastor and elders will consider the facts concerning an alleged abuse, weighing the evidence carefully. If it is clear that a criminal offence may have been committed, whether by a person outside the church or by a member, they will report the matter to the police and social services. In cases where the facts are less clear and there do not seem to be sufficient grounds of suspicion that an offence has occurred or that a child is at risk to warrant reporting the matter to the police or involving the local social services, the pastor and elders will seek the help of a respected, professional member of the church (eg: a solicitor or doctor) to investigate the allegations and to advise on whether there is sufficient evidence for the matter to be reported. A record will be kept of such incidents.

Appendix 2
Leaders' Duties in Relation to Discipline and Child Protection

Department leaders should receive a copy of this document before taking up their post.

(1) To be fully conversant with the 'Discipline and Child Protection Rules' given to all staff, and to ensure their full implementation in their department.

(2) To ensure that registers are being accurately kept at every meeting, and that full home address and telephone details for every child are recorded and available.

(3) To do everything in their power to prevent behaviour problems leading to children being physically handled. If a child is behaving in such a way as to provoke a disturbance, the department leader must withdraw the child and arrange for immediate home return if possible. The leader should inform the parents of the problem and ask them not to send the child for a few weeks, until it is clear his or her behaviour will improve.

(4) To record details of any accident or other incident in the site logbook (see below).

(5) To carefully note details of any concerns reported by a member of staff that a child may be suffering from the effects of some form of abuse, and to pass these details to the Sunday School coordinator on the same day. The leader is not to question the child or report the matter to the parents.

(6) If any incident occurs during which any member of staff appears to have lost their self-control in connection with the children, or involving any form of corporal discipline, the leader is to

take immediate action to restore a harmonious atmosphere and the safety of all the children. The details of the incident are to be recorded in the logbook and reported, *on the same day*, to the Sunday School coordinator, or a Tabernacle elder.

(7) To ensure that any child removed from a lesson for bad behaviour or ill health is cared for by a responsible adult until he/she can be taken home.

(8) To ensure that every meeting begins and ends on time so that parents' expectations for the collection and return of their children are met.

(9) To maintain order without frightening words, threats or physical intervention, except to separate fighting children, or to restrain a child from potential harm.

(10) To ensure that every child is kept safely on the premises until taken home by Sunday School staff or collected by their parents.

(11) To liaise closely with other leaders to ensure consistent treatment of difficult children.

(12) To ensure that first-aid facilities are available, and that team members with first-aid skills are known to all staff.

(13) To report to the coordinator when the running of a meeting would involve failure to keep these rules, eg: through insufficient helpers or staff for transport.

The Logbook

In order to provide a record for future reference a logbook will be available for each site. The purpose of the logbook is to record details of:

(1) Any accidents involving the children.

(2) Any incidents resulting in the physical restraint of children.

(3) Any incidents resulting in the suspension of a member of staff.

(4) Children leaving the premises early.

(5) Children usually collected by a parent, who does not appear.

(6) The need to communicate with parents concerning behaviour problems.

(7) The need to report suspicions of child abuse to the Sunday School coordinator.

Note: Entries must be made in the logbook on the same day as any incident. Only incidents such as these should be recorded in the logbook.

Appendix 3
Discipline and Child Protection Rules
For All Sunday School Workers

The coordinator or church officers must ensure that all staff receive a copy of these rules before beginning their work.

General Discipline and Child Protection Aims

With large numbers of children being collected and brought to our Sunday Schools and weeknight meetings, behavioural problems are likely to arise. The golden rule in our supervision of children is **'Prevention is better than cure'**. Many problems can be avoided if staff are well prepared in advance, arrive before children (whenever possible), and are watchful and ready to avert potentially difficult situations.

These rules have the following aims:

- The welfare and protection of the children at all times.
- Maintenance of the good name of the Tabernacle and the Lord's work in the eyes of parents and children.
- The consistent presentation of a good example of Christian behaviour to the young.
- The prompt dealing with bad behaviour so that the atmosphere is not spoilt for other children.
- The advancement of children with behavioural problems by giving them an opportunity to overcome their problems with the concerned and patient support of Tabernacle staff.
- The safe return home of children in a dangerous neighbourhood.
- The prevention of uncoordinated and conflicting courses of action being taken by different staff members.

Discipline Guidelines

(1) Speak firmly but without ill temper and shouting to a misbehaving child. Make it clear that certain behaviour is unacceptable on our vehicles and in the building (eg: deliberate foul language, racist comments, violence to others, conduct likely to cause an accident, damage to property).

(2) It may be necessary to part two fighting children, or to direct miscreants with a firm hand to the vehicle or room where they are supposed to be. **In no circumstances should any member of staff strike a child, no matter how gently, as this constitutes criminal assault.**

(3) Report incidents *urgently* as follows:

All Sunday School staff including transport team – report to the child's department leader.

All weeknight meetings staff including transport team – report to the child's meeting leader.

(4) Be careful to cooperate with any plan of action decided on to deal with a problem.

(5) No member of the transport team or individual teacher should ever ban a child from attending Sunday School or weeknight meetings, or refuse transport. Only leaders are empowered to stand down children.

Child Protection

(1) In order to protect the children and staff from potential problems, staff should avoid being alone with a child in a place where they cannot be seen.

(2) If staff find themselves alone with a child, they must avoid physical contact.

(3) Staff and transport helpers should avoid giving lifts in cars to just one child. If unavoidable, the child should sit in the back of the car.

(4) All children must be taken home by a responsible adult unless collected by the family, or where a parent has agreed that the child can go home unaccompanied.

(5) If you suspect that a child is suffering from the effects of physical injury or sexual abuse, do not question the child or speak to the parent but, *without delay*, inform your department leader, who may have knowledge of previous problems and has guidance on action to be taken. Within an hour of the meeting or event at which the suspicion arose, make a written note of the details including any comment made by the child and pass this note to the department leader.

(6) If you have reason to believe that another worker is having an inadvisable level of physical contact with the children, or is reacting in an inappropriate or potentially violent manner to problems, you must report your concerns *immediately* to your department leader. If he or she cannot be spoken to, you must report to the Sunday School coordinator or a Tabernacle elder without delay.

Appendix 4
Sunday School Materials Available from Tabernacle Bookshop

Lessons for Life 1– 4
Sunday School teachers' notes by Jill Masters
All books paperback, illustrated
Book 1, 207 pages, ISBN 1 870855 07 8
Book 2, 207 pages, ISBN 1 870855 11 6
Book 3, 252 pages, ISBN 1 870855 15 9
Book 4, 252 pages, ISBN 1 870855 20 5

The Necessity of Sunday Schools
by Peter Masters and Malcolm H. Watts; 112 pages, paperback, ISBN 1 870855 13 2
A clarion call for the unique effectiveness of evangelistic Sunday schools. Proof that the Bible sanctions and commands child evangelism. Stimulation and encouragement for the opening or enlargement of Sunday Schools along with advice and help for workers.

Lessons for Life Visual Aids
Full-colour professional quality visual aid packs to accompany each *Lessons for Life* volume.
There are 92 to 100 sheets (A3 and A2) in each pack.

Lessons for Life Bible Learning Course
Take-home leaflets to accompany each book of *Lessons for Life* lessons. Outline picture for colouring by children, containing questions, hymn verse and daily Bible readings. Master copies to be photocopied for local use.

Supplement pack available for special events: Prizegiving, Christmas, Easter and Anniversary meetings as well as summer holidays.

Weeknight Term Topics

A4 folders containing outline talks and suggestions for a series of weeknight meeting talks for children and young people. Six have been published, others will be published shortly.

Topic 1   Why Believe in God?

Topic 2   The War of the World Against God's Word

Topic 3   The Bible, An Amazing Book

Topic 4   The Bible and Medicine

Topic 5   Prayer

Topic 6   Matters of Life and Death

Sunday School class registers

Registers following the calendar and academic year are available at cost price.

Hymn and chorus sheets

Sets of hymns, choruses and single hymn verses are currently available for local enlarging and photocopying.

Prizegiving suggestions

A large selection of Christian books recommended for prizes is available. A list with prices will be sent on request.

New year motto texts

Professionally designed A4 colouring sheets for local photocopying. Available at cost price.

Tabernacle Bookshop
Metropolitan Tabernacle
Elephant & Castle
London SE1 6SD
Website: www.TabernacleBookshop.org
E-mail: Bookshop@MetropolitanTabernacle.org
Tel: 020 7735 7076

Appendix 5
The Biblical Warrant for Child Evangelism

Our scriptural warrant derives from the following texts:

(1) Commands of Scripture to include children of unbelievers in our work

(a) 'Gather the people together, men, and women, and children, and thy *stranger* that is within thy gates, that they may hear, and that they may learn, and fear the Lord your God, and observe to do all the words of this law: and that their children, which *have not known any thing*, may hear, and learn to fear the Lord your God' *(Deuteronomy 31.12-13)*.

(b) Christ, speaking of children and using the parable of the one *lost* sheep, said: 'It is not the will of your Father which is in heaven, that one of these little ones should perish' *(Matthew 18.14)*.

(c) 'And he *[Jesus]* said unto them, Go ye into *all* the world, and preach the gospel to *every* creature' *(Mark 16.15)*.

(2) Scriptures assuring us that children, while young, can seek and find the Lord

(a) 'Those that seek me early shall find me' *(Proverbs 8.17)*; 'Whoso findeth me findeth life' *(Proverbs 8.35)*.

(b) Samuel said, 'Speak; for thy servant heareth' *(1 Samuel 3.10)*.

(c) Christ said, 'Suffer little children, and forbid them not, to come unto me: for of such is the kingdom of heaven' *(Matthew 19.14; Mark 10.14; Luke 18.16)*.

(d) 'Except ye be converted, and become as little children, ye shall not enter into the kingdom of heaven . . . and whoso shall receive one such little child in my name receiveth me' *(Matthew 18.3 & 5)*.

(e) 'From a *child* thou hast known the holy scriptures, which are able to make thee wise unto salvation through faith which is in Christ Jesus' *(2 Timothy 3.15)*.

(3) Scriptures which command us to include children in our plan of instruction

(a) 'And it shall come to pass, when your children shall say unto you, What mean ye by this service? that ye shall say . . .' *(Exodus 12.26-27).* See also *Exodus 12.8* and *14.*

(b) 'Only take heed to thyself, and keep thy soul diligently, lest thou forget the things which thine eyes have seen . . . but teach them thy sons, and thy sons' sons' *(Deuteronomy 4.9).*

(c) 'And ye shall teach them your children, speaking of them when thou sittest in thine house . . .' *(Deuteronomy 11.19).*

(d) 'My son, hear the instruction of thy father, and forsake not the law of thy mother' *(Proverbs 1.8).*

(e) 'Train up a child in the way he should go: and when he is old, he will not depart from it' *(Proverbs 22.6).*

(f) 'Tell ye your children of it, and let your children tell their children, and their children another generation' *(Joel 1.3).*

(g) 'Fathers . . . bring them *[your children]* up in the nurture and admonition of the Lord' *(Ephesians 6.4).*

(4) Warnings to those indifferent to the spiritual needs of children

(a) 'And when the chief priests and scribes saw the wonderful things that he did, and the children crying in the temple, and saying, Hosanna to the Son of David; they were sore displeased, and said unto him, Hearest thou what these say? And Jesus saith unto them, Yea; have ye never read, Out of the mouth of babes and sucklings thou hast perfected praise?' *(Matthew 21.15-16.)*

(b) 'Whoso shall offend one of these little ones which believe in me, it were better for him that a millstone were hanged about his neck, and that he were drowned in the depth of the sea . . . Take heed that ye despise not one of these little ones; for I say unto you, That in heaven their angels do always behold the face of my Father which is in heaven. For the Son of man is come to save that which was lost' *(Matthew 18.6, 10, 11).* Read *Matthew 18.1-14.*